LEADERSHIP PRACTICES INVENTORY [LPI]

Revised Second Edition

Participant's Workbook

James M. Kouzes

Barry Z. Posner, Ph.D.

JOSSEY-BASS/PFEIFFER
A Wiley Imprint
www.pfeiffer.com

Published by Jossey-Bass/Pfeiffer
A Wiley Imprint
989 Market Street, San Francisco, CA 94103-1741   www.pfeiffer.com   www.TheLeadershipChallenge.com

Jossey-Bass/Pfeiffer is a registered trademark of John Wiley & Sons, Inc.

ISBN: 0-7879-5653-8

Jossey-Bass books and products are available through most bookstores. To contact Jossey-Bass directly call our Customer Care Department within the U.S. at 800-956-7739, outside the U.S. at 317-572-3986 or fax 317-572-4002.

Jossey-Bass also publishes its books in a variety of electronic formats. Some content that appears in print may not be available in electronic books.

Printed in the United States of America

Printing 10 9 8 7 6 5 4 3

CONTENTS

CHAPTER 1

What You Will Gain from the LPI

There's a popular myth that only a lucky few can decipher the mystery of leadership. But we've been researching leadership for more than eighteen years, and our research has demonstrated consistently and conclusively that leadership is not a mystery. We've gathered a huge amount of data—from more than 4,000 cases and 200,000 surveys—showing that leadership is an observable, learnable set of practices.

After assessing all of this information, the conclusion we've come to is this: *Leadership is everyone's business.* Everyone must function as a leader at some time and in some arena—whether in an organization, an agency, a task force, a committee, a community group, or even a family setting—and everyone can learn to lead effectively. That's why we wrote a second edition of our foundational book, *The Leadership Challenge,* and why we've continued to develop and improve our assessment instrument, the *Leadership Practices Inventory (LPI),* beyond its original version. We wanted to provide enhanced educational and training tools that would help *liberate the leader in everyone.*

And now that you're about to complete the LPI process, you'll be working toward liberating the leader in yourself. Regardless of whether you're new to a leadership role or you've been leading others for years, we believe that you'll gain valuable insights about yourself and find practical, useful information that will enable you to realize your full leadership potential.

WHAT YOU CAN EXPECT

As a result of completing the LPI self-development process, you can expect to:

- Learn The Five Practices of Exemplary Leadership

- Receive valid and reliable feedback about your current use of these practices

- Find out how others perceive you

- Identify your leadership strengths and opportunities for improvement

- Find specific suggestions on how to improve in each of the five leadership practices

- Make action plans for continuing your leadership development

- Learn a process for discussing your feedback with others

WHAT'S IN THIS WORKBOOK

Here's what you'll find in this workbook:

- A brief explanation of the development of the LPI

- Descriptions of the five practices of exemplary leadership

- An explanation of how to analyze and interpret LPI feedback

- Questions that guide you through a detailed analysis of your own feedback

- More than 130 ways to improve your day-to-day use of the leadership practices

- Action-planning forms to complete so that you can direct your efforts to improve

- A suggested design for conducting a meeting with the people who gave you the gift of this feedback, so that you can learn even more from them

- A list of recommended reading that you can use to further your leadership development

WHAT WE WISH FOR YOU

We wish you continuing success as you strive to meet your own leadership challenges. You'll discover, as we did, that leadership is essential not only in your career but in all of your relationships with others. When people succeed in improving their use of the five leadership practices, they enhance their contributions to their organizations and to their families and communities as well. Eventually you'll be helping your constituents (your direct reports, coworkers, and colleagues) to liberate the leader in themselves, too.

We trust that the LPI will serve as a useful compass as you make your journey toward self-discovery and self-development. And we thank you for taking us along.

James M. Kouzes
San Jose, California
July 2000

Barry Z. Posner
Santa Clara, California
July 2000

CHAPTER 2

The Five Practices of Exemplary Leadership™

When we decided to research leadership, we chose not to focus on famous military or political leaders, CEOs of corporations, or those who make headlines. What we wanted to know was how ordinary people accomplished *extraordinary* things in organizations. These were the people, we believed, who could demonstrate that leadership was accessible to everyone. So we concentrated on folks whose daily lives consisted of such activities as leading projects, managing departments, starting small businesses, and promoting community-based campaigns.

We began by developing a questionnaire that we called the "Personal-Best Leadership Experience." Thousands of people completed the questionnaire, and we interviewed many more, using the questionnaire as a basis for our interviews. Each person was asked to select a project, program, or significant event that represented his or her "personal-best" leadership experience. Then the person answered specific questions about that experience. Here are some examples of the questions we used:

- What made you believe you could accomplish the results you wanted?

- What did you do to get other people involved in the project?

- What strategies did you use to encourage others to "stretch" in their efforts to meet project goals?

- What key lessons about leadership did you learn from the experience?

Despite the differences in people's individual stories, the personal-best leadership experiences that we read and listened to revealed similar patterns of action. We found that when leaders were at their personal best, they were:

1. Challenging the Process

2. Inspiring a Shared Vision

3. Enabling Others to Act

4. Modeling the Way

5. Encouraging the Heart

3

In the following paragraphs we've provided brief descriptions of these five practices. You'll find more information in Chapter 7.[1]

CHALLENGING THE PROCESS

Leaders *search for opportunities* to change the status quo. They look for innovative ways to improve the organization. In doing so, they *experiment and take risks*. And because leaders know that risk taking involves mistakes and failures, they accept the inevitable disappointments as learning opportunities.

INSPIRING A SHARED VISION

Leaders passionately believe that they can make a difference. They *envision the future,* creating an ideal and unique image of what the organization can become. Through their magnetism and quiet persuasion, leaders *enlist others* in their dreams. They breathe life into their visions and get people to see exciting possibilities for the future.

ENABLING OTHERS TO ACT

Leaders *foster collaboration* and build spirited teams. They actively involve others. Leaders understand that mutual respect is what sustains extraordinary efforts; they strive to create an atmosphere of trust and human dignity. They *strengthen others,* making each person feel capable and powerful.

MODELING THE WAY

Leaders establish principles concerning the way people (constituents, colleagues, and customers alike) should be treated and the way goals should be pursued. They create standards of excellence and then *set an example* for others to follow. Because the prospect of complex change can overwhelm people and stifle action, they set interim goals so that people can *achieve small wins* as they work toward larger objectives. They unravel bureaucracy when it impedes action; they put up signposts when people are unsure of where to go or how to get there; and they create opportunities for victory.

ENCOURAGING THE HEART

Accomplishing extraordinary things in organizations is hard work. To keep hope and determination alive, leaders *recognize contributions* that individuals make. In every winning team, the members need to share in the rewards of their efforts, so leaders *celebrate accomplishments*. They make people feel like heroes.

---

[1]*In addition, each practice is discussed at length in our book,* The Leadership Challenge: How to Keep Getting Extraordinary Things Done in Organizations, *published by Jossey-Bass, San Francisco, in 1995.*

CHAPTER 3

What the LPI Measures

The LPI provides you with information about your leadership behavior. It does not measure IQ, personality, style, or general management skills.

We designed the LPI to be used by multiple raters. By completing the LPI, you and several observers can give feedback on your use of the five leadership practices (Challenging the Process, Inspiring a Shared Vision, Enabling Others to Act, Modeling the Way, and Encouraging the Heart). The people selected as observers must be *only those who directly observe you* as a leader.

At a minimum, the observers should include your direct reports. The observers may also include your immediate manager and your coworkers (peers or colleagues). You may even want to include a couple of people outside your organization, such as key customers or vendors who have observed you closely in your leadership role. Before you distribute the LPI-Observer forms, here are some things you need to do:

1. Write your name on each observer form in *two places*: in the blank marked "Name of Leader" on the front page *and* in the same blank on the response sheet.

2. Check the appropriate box indicating each observer's relationship to you. *Do not write the observers' names on the response sheets.* There are boxes for Manager, Direct Report, Coworker, and Other. If you are including observers who don't fit in the manager, direct report, or coworker categories, check the Other box for these observers.

You'll complete the LPI-Self, and the observers you choose will complete the LPI-Observer. Both you and the observers will indicate how frequently you engage in each of thirty behaviors (six for each leadership practice). The inventory uses a ten-point frequency scale, where "1" indicates "almost never" and "10" indicates "almost always."

WHAT DIFFERENCE DOES THE LPI MAKE?

At this point you may be wondering "Do my scores on the LPI matter? Will it really make a difference if I use the LPI behaviors more often?" Although there are no universal, "right" answers when it comes to leadership, our research, and that of others who have used our instrument, consistently shows the same result: *The more frequently you demonstrate the behaviors included in the LPI, the more likely you will be seen as an effective leader.* Figure 1 offers more specific information on how people are perceived when they use LPI behaviors frequently.

People who frequently demonstrate LPI behaviors are seen as:

- Being more effective in meeting job-related demands

- Being more successful in representing their units to upper management

- Creating higher-performing teams

- Fostering loyalty and commitment

- Increasing motivational levels and willingness to work hard

- Reducing absenteeism, turnover, and dropout rates

- Possessing high degrees of personal credibility

FIGURE 1. Observers' Perceptions of People Who Frequently Use LPI Behaviors

CAN YOU COUNT ON THE LPI FEEDBACK?

Any good instrument should have sound psychometric properties—reliability and validity. In general, an instrument is "reliable" when it measures what it's supposed to measure; it's "valid" when it accurately predicts performance. When we were developing the LPI, we conducted a number of tests to determine whether the inventory had sound psychometric properties. Here's what we found:

The LPI is internally reliable. This means that the six statements pertaining to each leadership practice are highly correlated with one another.

Test-retest reliability is high. This means that scores from one administration of the LPI to another within a short time span (a few months) and without any significant intervening event (such as a leadership-training program) are consistent and stable.

The five scales are generally independent (statistically orthogonal). This means that the five scales—corresponding to the five leadership practices—don't all measure the same phenomenon. Instead, they measure five *different* practices, as they should.

The LPI has both face validity and predictive validity. "Face validity" means that the results make sense to people. "Predictive validity" means that the results are significantly correlated with various performance measures and can be used to make predictions about leadership effectiveness.

SHOULD YOUR SELF AND OBSERVER SCORES BE THE SAME?

Research indicates that trust in a leader is essential if other people are going to follow that person over time. One of the ways that trust is developed is through consistency in leader behavior. Therefore, the closer your view of yourself to the view others have of you, the more likely it is that others will trust you. In the ideal scenario, your self ratings would be consistent with your observer ratings.

In the real world, however, scores aren't always consistent. People may see you differently from the way you see yourself, and they also may differ among themselves as to how they see you. Here are just a few of the possible reasons for such discrepancies:

• Some people may not work with you face to face as often as others; therefore, they may rate you differently on the same behavior.

• Some people may not know you as well as others.

• You may really behave differently in different situations.

• People may differ in their expectations of you.

• Some people may attribute different meanings to the frequency terms used in the LPI. (For example, just how often is "fairly often"?)

The key issue is not whether your self and observer ratings are exactly the same, but whether people perceive consistency between what you say you do and what you actually do. The only way you can know whether that consistency exists is to elicit feedback, and one of the best ways to get that feedback is to use the LPI. Once you have pinpointed any inconsistencies, you can do something about them.

NOW WHAT DO YOU DO WITH THIS INFORMATION?

Feedback is useless unless you act on it. Consider this analogy: If your gas gauge tells you that your car is on empty and you keep driving until your car stalls in the middle of a freeway, is your gas gauge of any use? The LPI is like your gas gauge. It gives you accurate information, but you're the one who has to decide what to do with that information.

As mentioned before, we know from research that leadership consists of observable and learnable behaviors. Even if you're a highly experienced leader, you can improve your ability to lead if you:

- Receive feedback on your present use of the desired behaviors

- Observe positive models of those behaviors

- Set goals for yourself

- Practice the behaviors

- Ask for and receive updated feedback on your performance

- Set new goals

Of course, there's one more critical ingredient for self-improvement: *desire*. In order to get the most from your LPI feedback, you have to want to improve. It's a good idea to do an internal check to make sure you truly aspire to become a better leader than you are today.

CHAPTER 4

How to Analyze and Interpret LPI Feedback[2]

The purpose of Chapter 4 is to guide you through the process of analyzing a computer-generated LPI feedback report. After you review this chapter, you'll understand how the LPI results are organized and displayed and you'll be prepared to interpret your own feedback.

Your report will consist of a cover page plus fourteen pages of tables and graphs that present your self and observer ratings on all thirty LPI statements. In this chapter you'll find samples of six of those pages:

1. Summary page

2. Summary graph page

3. Percentile ranking page

4. LPI-behaviors ranking page

5. Individual-practice page for Challenging the Process

6. Individual-practice graph page for Challenging the Process

These six sample pages will show you how to read your entire report. They've been completed with a hypothetical leader's results, and we've provided a detailed explanation of the content of each page.

---

[2]*This chapter assumes that your LPI-Self and LPI-Observer forms have been computer scored and that you will receive a computer-generated report of your scores. If this isn't the case, you'll need to record self and observer scores on the grids provided in Appendix B. Even if you won't be receiving a computer-generated report, the practice feedback analysis in this chapter will help you to understand your scores.*

First let's take a look at the summary page (Figure 2).

LEADERSHIP PRACTICES INVENTORY

Profile for Jane Doe

Universal Widget
July 25, 2000

	SELF	LPI-OBSERVER RATINGS									
		AVG	AGR	M1	M2	D1	D2	C1	C2	O1	O2
ENABLING OTHERS TO ACT	43	41.0	L	57	52	18	35	35	33	55	43
ENCOURAGING THE HEART	43	40.8	H	40	42	41	40	35	32	50	46
MODELING THE WAY	48	40.4	M	33	34	37	33	38	47	56	45
INSPIRING A SHARED VISION	33	36.5	L	24	20	45	30	34	41	51	47
CHALLENGING THE PROCESS	46	33.9	L	42	35	22	22	16	28	57	49

AVG = Average of all LPI Observer ratings

AGR = Degree of consistency between observer scores, with H = High,
M = Moderate, and L = Low degree of consistency or agreement

M = Managers	D = Direct Reports
C = Coworkers	O = Others

FIGURE 2. Sample Summary Page

SUMMARY PAGE

Five Practices

The first or far-left column of the summary page lists the names of the five practices. Although we described the five practices earlier in the sequence of Challenging the Process, Inspiring a Shared Vision, Enabling Others to Act, Modeling the Way, and Encouraging the Heart, you'll notice that on the summary page the practices are displayed in the order of highest to lowest average observer scores.

We've designed the page in this way so that you can quickly find the areas that observers perceive to be your strengths as well as the areas they perceive to be your opportunities for improvement. This information will prove useful later in the LPI feedback process, as you begin to make self-development plans.

Self Rating

The scores in the "Self" column represent the sum of your LPI-Self responses to the six statements about each of the five leadership practices. The score for each practice can range from a high of 60 to a low of 6.

LPI-Observer Ratings

Under the heading "LPI-Observer Ratings" are several columns of scores:

"AVG" (average). The numbers in this column are the averages—practice by practice—of all of the observers' ratings. The average can range from a high of 60 to a low of 6.

"AGR" (agreement). The letters in this column indicate the level of agreement between all of the observers' ratings, practice by practice. The calculation of the AGR score is based on the standard deviation of the observers' ratings. Standard deviation is a measure of the variation around the calculated average of the scores. Kouzes and Posner have established a standard deviation range based on their database of respondents' results for each of the practices. AGR scores with a standard deviation within this range are considered (M)oderate agreement. Standard deviations exceeding this range represent a high variation in the results and are thus considered (L)ow agreement. Standard deviations that are below this range represent very consistent results and are thus considered (H)igh agreement. The actual values for these cutoff points are:

	High	Moderate	Low
Challenging the Process:	0 to 4.43	4.44 to 13.28	13.29 and above
Inspiring a Shared Vision:	0 to 5.19	5.20 to 15.55	15.56 and above
Enabling Others to Act:	0 to 4.06	4.07 to 12.16	12.17 and above
Modeling the Way:	0 to 4.12	4.13 to 12.35	12.36 and above
Encouraging the Heart:	0 to 4.98	4.99 to 14.93	14.94 and above

"M" (your manager), "D" (direct report), "C" (coworker), and "O" (other). The observer feedback you receive isn't identified by the names of the people who generated it. But these columns tell you what categories the observers were assigned to and how many people were in each category.

The sample summary page has data in all possible observer columns. But when you receive your report, you may or may not have all columns, depending on several factors:

- Whether all categories of observers completed an LPI-Observer form for you

- Whether you wanted observer feedback from people who simply didn't fit in the "M," "D," or "C" categories

- Whether the numbers of observers are large enough to separate into categories (minimum of two observers per category—with the exception of your manager—to protect the observers' anonymity)

- Whether you wanted your observer data separated into categories

For example, let's assume that you gave LPI-Observer forms only to your direct reports and you marked the "Direct Report" box on every observer response sheet. In this case you'll have feedback from D1, D2, D3, and so on, but you won't have feedback from your manager, your coworkers, or other observers.

In another case, let's say that you wanted feedback from your manager, from several direct reports, and from a couple of coworkers. But you also wanted feedback from a couple of key customers who observe you frequently in your leadership role. The feedback from those customers wouldn't be appropriate for the "M," "D," or "C" categories, so it will be reported in the "O" columns.

Now let's assume that you gave an observer form to only one direct report and another to only one coworker and you marked the appropriate box for each. You still won't have coworker and direct-report feedback, because the minimum number of people per category wasn't met. Instead, the data from these two people will be reported in the "O" columns.

You may even have decided at the outset that you didn't want your observer data separated into categories. In this case all of your data will be reported in the "O" columns.

As you can see, the "O" (other) designation can function either as a catchall or a default category.

If your summary page doesn't have data from all categories of observers, the other portions of your feedback report also won't have such data.

The codes for individual observers are consistent throughout your report: D1 is always the same direct report, C1 is always the same coworker, and so on. The numbers that appear in each column below the category heading on the summary page are the scores per practice for that observer. Again, a score can range from a high of 60 to a low of 6.

SUMMARY GRAPH PAGE

Next look at Figure 3. This page has a set of bar graphs for each of the five practices, listed in the order of highest to lowest average observer scores. The corresponding numerical scores appear in the right column. Self bars and scores are displayed first, followed by bars and scores for observers. Each observer bar represents the *average* score for that category, so the set of bars for each practice illustrates how the different categories of scores compare.

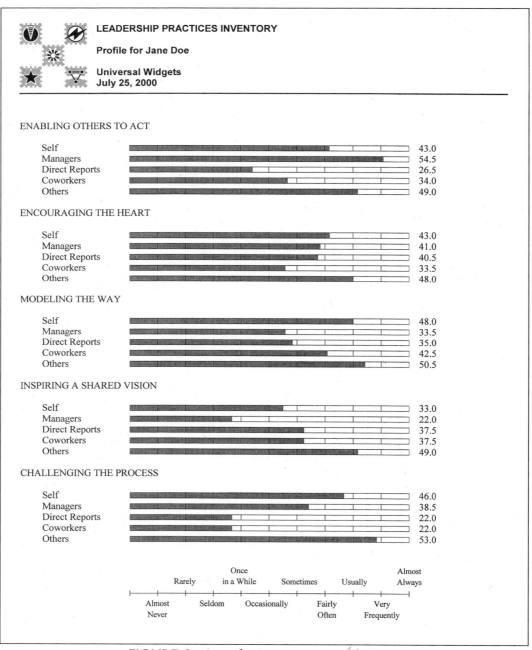

FIGURE 3. Sample Summary Graph Page

In Figure 3 there are bars for all possible sources of data: self, manager, direct reports, coworkers, and others. When you receive your report, you may or may not have all of these bars, depending on whether your observers have been divided into categories and which categories you have.

Interpreting the Summary Information

Take a few moments to study the sample summary—both the numerical ratings in Figure 2 and the bar graphs in Figure 3—and analyze the hypothetical leader's feedback. Think about how you would answer these questions:

1. How does the leader rate herself? In which practice does she give herself the highest rating? The second? Third? Fourth? The lowest rating? These ratings indicate areas that she considers to be her strengths and areas in which she might consider improvement.

2. In which practice do the observers give her the highest rating? The second? Third? Fourth? The lowest rating? These ratings indicate what the observers, on average, consider to be her strengths and areas for improvement.

3. What similarities do you find in the self and average observer ratings with regard to strengths and areas for improvement? What differences do you find? What factors might explain the differences?

4. Look at the numerical ratings given by *individual observers*. How does the leader's manager rate her? Compare the individual direct reports to one another, the individual coworkers to one another, and the individual other observers to one another. Do the people in each of these observer categories generally agree or disagree with one another? What are the similarities within each category? What are the differences? What might account for the differences?

5. Analyze the numerical ratings and bar charts by *categories*. Compare the self, manager, average direct-report, average coworker, and average other-observer ratings to one another. What areas of agreement and disagreement do you find? What might you conclude from your findings?

PERCENTILE RANKING PAGE

Figure 4 is a sample of the page that compares your scores to those of all people in the LPI database. The percentile rankings have been determined by the percentage of those people who have scored at or below a given number. For example, let's say that your score for Challenging the Process is at the 70th percentile line. This means that you scored higher in that practice than 70 percent of all of the people who have taken the LPI. In other words, you are in the top 30 percent for Challenging the Process.

The numbers along the left margin in Figure 4 represent percentile rankings in increments of ten. We've divided the graph into three segments with horizontal lines, representing the top, middle, and bottom third of the scores. From left to right are columns for Challenging, Inspiring, Enabling, Modeling, and Encouraging. Your own percentile rankings for these practices will be plotted on the graph and connected with lines.

Here's what the different lines illustrate: "S" = self ratings, "M" = your manager's ratings, "D" = average ratings for direct reports, "C" = average ratings for coworkers, "O" = average ratings for other observers.

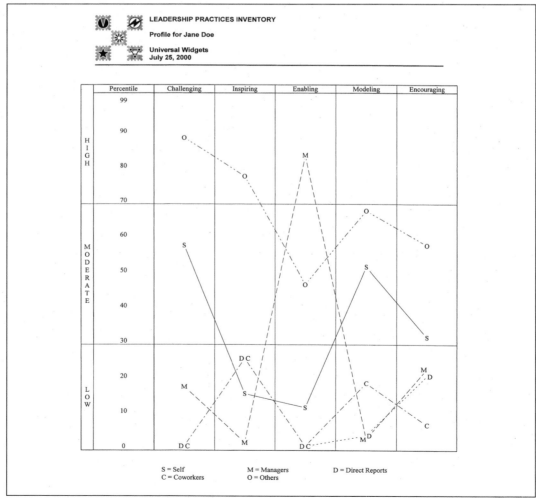

FIGURE 4. Sample Percentile Ranking Page

Your own percentile ranking page may be different. If you don't have observer categories, you'll see two lines: (1) one marked "S" for self and (2) one marked "O," representing responses from all of the people who completed LPI-Observer forms for you.

Essentially, the percentile rankings are benchmarking numbers that provide a context for your scores. Our studies indicate that a "high" score is one at the 70th percentile or above, whereas a "low" score is one at the 30th percentile or below. A score that falls between 31 and 69 percent would be considered "moderate."

Analyzing the Percentile Ranking Page

Let's examine the hypothetical leader's percentile rankings in Figure 4 and see what they reveal. Think about how you would answer the following questions:

1. First look at the leader's self scores, designated by the line marked "S." In which percentile does each of the five practices fall? How do her percentiles compare with those of others in the LPI database? In which areas does she believe she's strong? In which areas does she believe there's room for improvement?

2. Next look at the scores from the leader's manager, designated by the line marked "M." What are the percentiles for each of the five practices? How do these percentiles compare with those in the LPI database? What does the leader's manager consider to be her strengths? What does the manager consider to be her opportunities for improvement?

3. Now look at the remaining scores: the direct reports' (the line marked "D"), the coworkers' (the line marked "C"), and the other observers' (the line marked "O"). How do these percentiles compare with those in the LPI database? What do these different categories of observers believe to be the leader's strengths? What do they believe to be areas in which she needs to improve?

4. Compare the self line with the lines for the different categories of observers. Are they parallel or do they intersect? If the lines are parallel, then the leader and the different categories of observers basically agree about her strengths and opportunities for improvement. If the lines intersect, then the leader and the observers disagree. In the case of this leader, where is there agreement? Where is there disagreement?

5. Look at the degrees of distance between the self line and the different observer lines. These distances illustrate the areas of agreement and disagreement between self and observers. Are this leader's self and observer lines close together or far apart? Where are there similar scores? Where are the differences most pronounced?

LPI-BEHAVIORS RANKING PAGE

Figure 5 is a sample of the LPI-behaviors ranking page. This page displays ratings for each of the thirty behavioral statements, which are listed in abbreviated form.

The statements are ranked in order from highest to lowest average observer score. In addition, there's a horizontal line isolating the ten lowest scores.

For purposes of comparison, the self ratings are displayed next to the average observer ratings. A score marked with an *asterisk* (*) indicates that the average observer score and the self score differ by more than plus or minus 1.5.

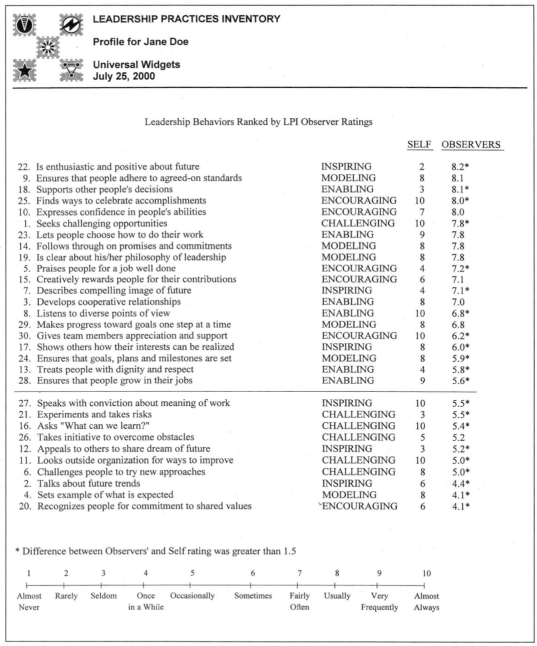

LEADERSHIP PRACTICES INVENTORY

Profile for Jane Doe

Universal Widgets
July 25, 2000

Leadership Behaviors Ranked by LPI Observer Ratings

		SELF	OBSERVERS
22. Is enthusiastic and positive about future	INSPIRING	2	8.2*
9. Ensures that people adhere to agreed-on standards	MODELING	8	8.1
18. Supports other people's decisions	ENABLING	3	8.1*
25. Finds ways to celebrate accomplishments	ENCOURAGING	10	8.0*
10. Expresses confidence in people's abilities	ENCOURAGING	7	8.0
1. Seeks challenging opportunities	CHALLENGING	10	7.8*
23. Lets people choose how to do their work	ENABLING	9	7.8
14. Follows through on promises and commitments	MODELING	8	7.8
19. Is clear about his/her philosophy of leadership	MODELING	8	7.8
5. Praises people for a job well done	ENCOURAGING	4	7.2*
15. Creatively rewards people for their contributions	ENCOURAGING	6	7.1
7. Describes compelling image of future	INSPIRING	4	7.1*
3. Develops cooperative relationships	ENABLING	8	7.0
8. Listens to diverse points of view	ENABLING	10	6.8*
29. Makes progress toward goals one step at a time	MODELING	8	6.8
30. Gives team members appreciation and support	ENCOURAGING	10	6.2*
17. Shows others how their interests can be realized	INSPIRING	8	6.0*
24. Ensures that goals, plans and milestones are set	MODELING	8	5.9*
13. Treats people with dignity and respect	ENABLING	4	5.8*
28. Ensures that people grow in their jobs	ENABLING	9	5.6*
27. Speaks with conviction about meaning of work	INSPIRING	10	5.5*
21. Experiments and takes risks	CHALLENGING	3	5.5*
16. Asks "What can we learn?"	CHALLENGING	10	5.4*
26. Takes initiative to overcome obstacles	CHALLENGING	5	5.2
12. Appeals to others to share dream of future	INSPIRING	3	5.2*
11. Looks outside organization for ways to improve	CHALLENGING	10	5.0*
6. Challenges people to try new approaches	CHALLENGING	8	5.0*
2. Talks about future trends	INSPIRING	6	4.4*
4. Sets example of what is expected	MODELING	8	4.1*
20. Recognizes people for commitment to shared values	ENCOURAGING	6	4.1*

* Difference between Observers' and Self rating was greater than 1.5

1	2	3	4	5	6	7	8	9	10
Almost Never	Rarely	Seldom	Once in a While	Occasionally	Sometimes	Fairly Often	Usually	Very Frequently	Almost Always

FIGURE 5. Sample LPI-Behaviors Ranking Page

The thirty LPI statements specify behaviors that, according to our research, exemplify the five practices. The practice to which each statement applies is listed on the LPI-behaviors ranking page. The feedback on specific behaviors will help you decide how to target your improvement efforts and how to build on your strengths. Also, you'll want to review your scores from time to time, and this page can serve as a quick reference for that purpose.

The numbers in the "Self" and "Observers" columns on the right can range from 10.0 to 1.0, because each behavior was rated on a frequency scale from 10 to 1:

$$10 = \text{Almost Always}$$
$$9 = \text{Very Frequently}$$
$$8 = \text{Usually}$$
$$7 = \text{Fairly Often}$$
$$6 = \text{Sometimes}$$
$$5 = \text{Occasionally}$$
$$4 = \text{Once in a While}$$
$$3 = \text{Seldom}$$
$$2 = \text{Rarely}$$
$$1 = \text{Almost Never}$$

Interpreting the LPI-Behaviors Ranking Page

Let's analyze the LPI-behaviors ranking page for our hypothetical leader. How would you answer the following questions?

1. First look at the highest-rated items in Figure 5. Which specific leadership behaviors does this leader exhibit most often? These behaviors are her strengths.

2. Next look at the lowest-rated items. The ten behaviors that this leader exhibits least often are listed below the horizontal line. Which behaviors are they? These behaviors represent opportunities for improvement, regardless of their scores.

3. Do you see items from one practice that form a cluster? If three or more items form a cluster at the lower end of the scale, then it's important to pay attention to that practice as a whole rather than just as single behaviors.

4. Which items are marked with an asterisk (*)? These items warrant further investigation to find out why agreement between self and observers is so low.

5. What conclusions can you draw from this LPI-behaviors ranking page? Given the information on this page, where would you suggest that the leader begin her development planning?

INDIVIDUAL-PRACTICE PAGE FOR CHALLENGING THE PROCESS

The LPI feedback report includes two pages for *each* of the five leadership practices. These pages, the individual-practice page and the individual-practice graph page, follow the formats of the summary page and the summary graph page, respectively. We've included samples illustrating the hypothetical leader's results for Challenging the Process. Let's look at the first of the two pages, the individual-practice page (Figure 6), and see what it tells us.

CHALLENGING THE PROCESS

Profile for Jane Doe

Universal Widgets
July 25, 2000

LEADERSHIP BEHAVIOR	SELF	LPI-OBSERVER RATINGS								
		AVG	M1	M2	D1	D2	C1	C2	O1	O2
1. Seeks challenging opportunities	10	7.8	10	10	10	10	3	1	9	9
21. Experiments and takes risks	3	5.5	8	8	3	3	1	4	10	7
16. Asks "What can we learn?"	10	5.4	7	4	4	4	1	3	10	10
26. Takes initiative to overcome obstacles	5	5.3	5	9	1	1	1	10	10	5
11. Looks outside organization for ways to improve	10	5.0	9	1	1	1	1	9	9	9
6. Challenges people to try new approaches	8	5.0	3	3	3	3	9	1	9	9
CUMULATIVE RATINGS:	46	33.9	42	35	22	22	16	28	57	49

1	2	3	4	5	6	7	8	9	10
Almost Never	Rarely	Seldom	Once in a While	Occasionally	Sometimes	Fairly Often	Usually	Very Frequently	Almost Always

FIGURE 6. Sample Individual-Practice Page for Challenging the Process

Leadership Behavior

The first or far-left column is labeled "Leadership Behavior." Each numbered item in this column is an abbreviated form of an LPI statement related to the practice. As you can see in Figure 6, items 1, 6, 11, 16, 21, and 26 relate to Challenging the Process.

On each individual-practice page, the abbreviated statements are listed in the order of highest to lowest average observer scores. This order of display gives you a quick look at the behaviors that others perceive to be your greatest strengths and your greatest opportunities for improvement within that particular practice—information that you'll need when you're making self-development plans.

Self Rating

The numbers in the "Self" column are the scores you gave yourself for the individual items. Because the rating scale ranges from a high of 10 to a low of 1, your individual scores can range from 10 to 1.

LPI-Observer Ratings

As is the case with the summary page, several types of observer scores are listed in the "LPI-Observer Ratings" column:

"AVG" (average). The numbers in this column, which can range from 10 to 1, are the item-by-item averages of all of the observers' ratings.

"M" (your manager), "D" (direct report), "C" (coworker), and "O" (other). The observer feedback on the individual-practice page, like that on the summary page, is identified by category and tells you how many people in each category submitted an LPI-Observer form.

As is the case with the sample summary page, the sample individual-practice page has data in all possible observer columns. But your own individual-practice pages may or may not have all of this data, depending on your circumstances.

Keep in mind that the codes for individual observers are consistent throughout your feedback report. D1, for example, on each individual-practice page is the same person designated as D1 on your summary page. Again, a single observer score can range from 10 to 1.

INDIVIDUAL-PRACTICE GRAPH PAGE
FOR CHALLENGING THE PROCESS

Figure 7 is a sample of the second of the two feedback pages for each practice, the individual-practice graph page. This page displays a set of bar graphs and corresponding numerical scores for each of the six statements that pertain to that practice. The statements are listed in order of highest to lowest average observer score.

Self bars and scores appear first, followed by observer bars and average scores. Again, your report may not reflect some types of observer data.

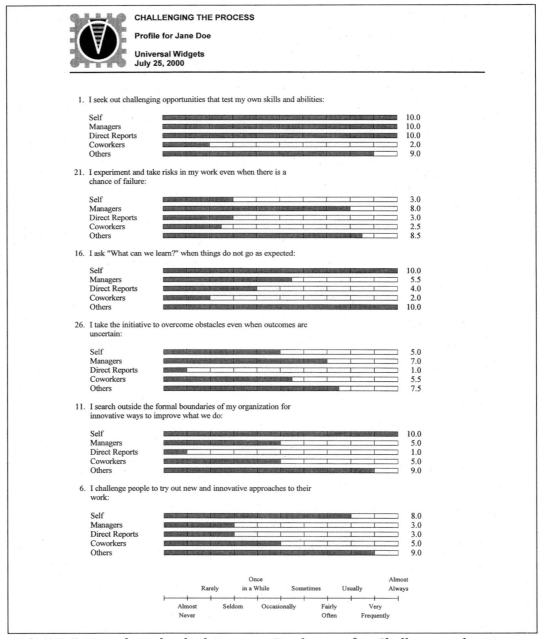

FIGURE 7. Sample Individual-Practice Graph Page for Challenging the Process

Interpreting the Sample Pages for Challenging the Process

Let's examine both sample pages (Figures 6 and 7) and see what we can determine about the hypothetical leader's use of Challenging the Process. Think about how you would answer these questions:

1. How does this leader rate herself on the six items? On which item does she give herself the first or highest rating? The second? Third? Fourth? Fifth? The lowest rating? These ratings indicate her own opinions about the areas that are her strengths and the areas that represent opportunities for improvement.

2. On average, how do the observers rate her? What item has the highest rating? The second? Third? Fourth? Fifth? The lowest rating?

3. Are the self and average observer ratings similar? Where are there differences in perception? What might explain the differences?

4. Examine the ratings given by *individual observers*. How does the leader's manager rate her? Also compare the individual direct reports to one another, the individual coworkers to one another, and the individual other observers to one another. Do the people in each of these observer categories generally agree or disagree with one another? What are the similarities within each category? What are the differences? What might account for the differences?

5. Analyze the numerical ratings and bar charts by *categories*. Compare the self, manager, average direct-report, average coworker, and average other ratings to one another. What areas of agreement and disagreement do you find? What might you conclude from your findings?

CHAPTER 5

Interpreting Your Own LPI Feedback[3]

Now that you've practiced analyzing a hypothetical leader's LPI feedback, you're ready to analyze and interpret your own feedback report. As explained in Chapter 4, you may or may not have scores from all categories of observers, depending on several factors. And if your observers were not divided into categories, your report will have only self ("S") and other ("O") information. When you find questions in this chapter dealing with observer categories that you don't have, ignore them.

Keep in mind that you'll be using your analysis of the feedback (your answers to the questions in this chapter) as a foundation for your self-development plans. As a result, in addition to answering the questions, you should jot down notes about any additional information you'd like to have from observers. If you have time, you might also want to make brief notes about additional conclusions you can draw, issues or implications you should consider, and actions you might consider taking.

First you'll work through the data pertaining to your overall feedback. Then you'll go through the five individual practices one by one.

---

[3]*This chapter assumes that you have received a computer-generated LPI feedback report. If this isn't the case and you haven't yet scored your LPI-Self and LPI-Observer forms, turn to Appendix B and follow the instructions for scoring. Then work through this chapter, answering as many questions as you can.*

YOUR SUMMARY PAGE AND SUMMARY GRAPH PAGE

Open your feedback report to the two pages that summarize your scores: the summary page and the summary graph page. Examine the feedback and write answers in the spaces provided.

1. First look at the ratings you gave yourself.

   • In which practice do you have the highest rating?

   • The second?

   • Third?

   • Fourth?

   • Fifth?

   • According to the ratings you gave yourself, what are your strengths?

   • According to your self ratings, what are the areas in which you might consider making improvements?

2. Now look at the average observer ratings.

- In which practice did the observers give you the highest rating?

- The second?

- Third?

- Fourth?

- Fifth?

- What do the observers indicate are your strengths?

- What do the observers indicate are areas in which you need to improve?

3. Next compare the ratings you gave yourself to the average observer ratings.

- Do you and the observers perceive your strengths to be the same or different? Where are the similarities and differences? What might explain the differences?

- What about the areas in which you need to improve? Do you and the observers have the same or different perceptions? Where are the similarities and differences? What might explain the differences?

4. Examine the numerical ratings given by *individual observers*.

• How did your manager rate you for each practice?

• Compare the individual direct reports (D1, D2, etc.) to one another, the individual coworkers (C1, C2, etc.) to one another, and the individual other observers (O1, O2, etc.) to one another. *(If you don't have separate observer categories, just compare your observers—O1, O2, etc.—to one another.)* In each category, where is there agreement *among the individuals?*

• Where is there disagreement?

• What can you conclude from this information?

5. Analyze the numerical ratings and bar charts by *categories*. Compare the self, manager, average direct-report, average coworker, and average other-observer ratings to one another. *(If you don't have separate observer categories, skip this item.)*

• What are the similarities *between categories?*

• What are the differences?

• What can you conclude from your findings? Consider the information, for example, in terms of who's closest to you: Do your manager and your direct reports tend to be in greater agreement with each other than those observer groups whose relationship is more distant?

YOUR PERCENTILE RANKING PAGE

Open your feedback report to the percentile ranking page. This is the page that offers you a way of benchmarking yourself against a cross-section of the leadership population—all of the people who make up the LPI database.

The "S" line illustrates the scores you gave yourself. If you have scores from all categories of observers, you'll have lines marked "M" for manager, "D" for direct reports, "C" for coworkers, and "O" for other observers. If you don't have observer categories, you'll see two lines: (1) one marked "S" for self and (2) one marked "O," representing responses from all of the people who completed LPI-Observer forms for you.

Examine the page and write answers to the following questions:

1. First look at the "S" line illustrating the ratings you gave yourself.

- In which percentile does each practice fall?

Challenging	Inspiring	Enabling	Modeling	Encouraging
_____	_____	_____	_____	_____

- In which areas are your self ratings strong, compared to others in the database?

- In which areas do your self ratings indicate that you have greater opportunities for improvement than others in the database?

- How does this information compare to what you learned about your self ratings from the summary page and the summary graph page? Are there any surprises? If so, what are they?

2. Now look at the lines designating the observer scores.

   • In which percentiles are your scores for each observer category? *(If you don't have separate observer categories, record the percentiles for all observers in the row marked "O.")*

	Challenging	Inspiring	Enabling	Modeling	Encouraging
M (Manager)	_____	_____	_____	_____	_____
D (Direct Reports)	_____	_____	_____	_____	_____
C (Coworkers)	_____	_____	_____	_____	_____
O (Other Observers)	_____	_____	_____	_____	_____

   • Where is there agreement among the observer categories about your strengths and opportunities for improvement, compared to others in the LPI database?

   • Where is there disagreement?

   • What does this information indicate to you?

3. Compare your self line to your observer lines.

- Are they parallel or do they intersect?

- Are they close together or far apart?

- Where are the greatest differences?

- Would you say, in general, that you *are* or *are not* in agreement with the observers?

YOUR LPI-BEHAVIORS RANKING PAGE

Open your feedback report to the LPI-behaviors ranking page. Remember that on this page the items, which are abbreviations of the statements in the LPI, are ranked in order according to average observer rating. Read the feedback carefully and answer the following questions:

1. First look at the highest-ranked items (your strengths). Which specific behaviors are they?

2. Now look at the lowest-ranked items (your opportunities for improvement).

   • Which specific behaviors are they?

   • Examine the lowest-ranked items to see whether you have three or more from one practice. If so, then you need to pay attention to that practice as a whole, rather than just as individual behaviors. Is this the case for you? If so, which practice is involved?

3. Compare your self ratings to the average observer ratings.

- In general, would you say that they're in agreement?

- Look at any items marked with an asterisk (*). The asterisk indicates that the self score and the average observer score differ by more than plus or minus 1.5. In other words, agreement between self and observers is low. Which items on your page are marked with an asterisk? (Later you'll want to look at the more detailed item feedback for each practice to gain a better understanding of any sources of low agreement.)

4. Given the data on this page, consider how you might approach your development planning. Where would you begin? With which practice?

YOUR FEEDBACK FOR CHALLENGING THE PROCESS

Open your feedback report to the two pages on Challenging the Process. Review your feedback and answer the questions following the boxed statements. *(Skip questions as necessary if you don't have certain categories of observers.)*

The Six LPI Statements for Challenging the Process

  1. I seek out challenging opportunities that test my own skills and abilities.

  6. I challenge people to try out new and innovative approaches to their work.

11. I search outside the formal boundaries of my organization for innovative ways to improve what we do.

16. I ask "What can we learn?" when things do not go as expected.

21. I experiment and take risks even where there is a chance of failure.

26. I take the initiative to overcome obstacles even when outcomes are uncertain.

I. Self Ratings

• For which behavior do you have the highest rating?

• The second?

• Third?

• Fourth?

• Fifth?

• Sixth?

• According to your self ratings, which behaviors are your strengths?

• Which behaviors warrant improvement?

2. Average Observer Ratings

• For which behavior did the observers give you the highest rating?

• The second?

• Third?

• Fourth?

• Fifth?

• Sixth?

• Which behaviors do observers indicate are your strengths?

• Which do they indicate are opportunities for improvement?

3. Comparison of Self Ratings to Average Observer Ratings

• What are the similarities?

• What are the differences? What might explain them?

4. Analysis of Individual Observer Ratings

• How does your manager rate you in each of the six behaviors?

• Compare the individual direct reports to one another, the individual coworkers to one another, and the individual other observers to one another. What are the similarities *within each category?*

• What are the differences? What might account for them?

5. Analysis of Ratings and Bar Charts by Categories

• Compare the self, manager, average direct-report, average coworker, and average other-observer ratings to one another. Where do you see similarities *between categories?*

• Where do you see differences?

• What can you conclude from your findings?

YOUR FEEDBACK FOR
INSPIRING A SHARED VISION

Open your feedback report to the two pages on Inspiring a Shared Vision. Review your feedback and answer the questions following the boxed statements. *(Skip questions as necessary if you don't have certain categories of observers.)*

The Six LPI Statements for Inspiring a Shared Vision

2. I talk about future trends that will influence how our work gets done.

7. I describe a compelling image of what our future could be like.

12. I appeal to others to share an exciting dream of the future.

17. I show others how their long-term interests can be realized by enlisting in a common vision.

22. I am contagiously enthusiastic and positive about future possibilities.

27. I speak with genuine conviction about the higher meaning and purpose of our work.

I. Self Ratings

• For which behavior do you have the highest rating?

• The second?

• Third?

• Fourth?

- Fifth?

- Sixth?

- According to your self ratings, which behaviors are your strengths?

- Which behaviors warrant improvement?

2. Average Observer Ratings

- For which behavior did the observers give you the highest rating?

- The second?

- Third?

- Fourth?

- Fifth?

- Sixth?

• Which behaviors do observers indicate are your strengths?

• Which do they indicate are opportunities for improvement?

3. Comparison of Self Ratings to Average Observer Ratings

• What are the similarities?

• What are the differences? What might explain them?

4. Analysis of Individual Observer Ratings

• How does your manager rate you in each of the six behaviors?

• Compare the individual direct reports to one another, the individual coworkers to one another, and the individual other observers to one another. What are the similarities *within each category?*

• What are the differences? What might account for them?

5. Analysis of Ratings and Bar Charts by Categories

• Compare the self, manager, average direct-report, average coworker, and average other-observer ratings to one another. Where do you see similarities *between categories?*

• Where do you see differences?

• What can you conclude from your findings?

YOUR FEEDBACK FOR ENABLING OTHERS TO ACT

Open your feedback report to the two pages on Enabling Others to Act. Review your feedback and answer the questions following the boxed statements. (*Skip questions as necessary if you don't have certain categories of observers.*)

The Six LPI Statements for Enabling Others to Act

3. I develop cooperative relationships among the people I work with.

8. I actively listen to diverse points of view.

13. I treat others with dignity and respect.

18. I support the decisions that people make on their own.

23. I give people a great deal of freedom and choice in deciding how to do their work.

28. I ensure that people grow in their jobs by learning new skills and developing themselves.

I. Self Ratings

• For which behavior do you have the highest rating?

• The second?

• Third?

• Fourth?

• Fifth?

• Sixth?

• According to your self ratings, which behaviors are your strengths?

• Which behaviors warrant improvement?

2. Average Observer Ratings

• For which behavior did the observers give you the highest rating?

• The second?

• Third?

• Fourth?

• Fifth?

• Sixth?

• Which behaviors do observers indicate are your strengths?

• Which do they indicate are opportunities for improvement?

3. Comparison of Self Ratings to Average Observer Ratings

• What are the similarities?

• What are the differences? What might explain them?

4. Analysis of Individual Observer Ratings

• How does your manager rate you in each of the six behaviors?

• Compare the individual direct reports to one another, the individual coworkers to one another, and the individual other observers to one another. What are the similarities *within each category*?

• What are the differences? What might account for them?

5. Analysis of Ratings and Bar Charts by Categories

• Compare the self, manager, average direct-report, average coworker, and average other-observer ratings to one another. Where do you see similarities *between categories?*

• Where do you see differences?

• What can you conclude from your findings?

YOUR FEEDBACK FOR MODELING THE WAY

Open your feedback report to the two pages on Modeling the Way. Review your feedback and answer the questions following the boxed statements. *(Skip questions as necessary if you don't have certain categories of observers.)*

The Six LPI Statements for Modeling the Way

4. I set a personal example of what I expect from others.

9. I spend time and energy on making certain that the people I work with adhere to the principles and standards that we have agreed on.

14. I follow through on the promises and commitments that I make.

19. I am clear about my philosophy of leadership.

24. I make certain that we set achievable goals, make concrete plans, and establish measurable milestones for the projects and programs that we work on.

29. I make progress toward goals one step at a time.

I. Self Ratings

• For which behavior do you have the highest rating?

• The second?

• Third?

• Fourth?

• Fifth?

• Sixth?

• According to your self ratings, which behaviors are your strengths?

• Which behaviors warrant improvement?

2. Average Observer Ratings

• For which behavior did the observers give you the highest rating?

• The second?

• Third?

• Fourth?

• Fifth?

• Sixth?

• Which behaviors do observers indicate are your strengths?

• Which do they indicate are opportunities for improvement?

3. Comparison of Self Ratings to Average Observer Ratings

• What are the similarities?

• What are the differences? What might explain them?

4. Analysis of Individual Observer Ratings

• How does your manager rate you in each of the six behaviors?

• Compare the individual direct reports to one another, the individual coworkers to one another, and the individual other observers to one another. What are the similarities *within each category*?

• What are the differences? What might account for them?

5. Analysis of Ratings and Bar Charts by Categories

• Compare the self, manager, average direct-report, average coworker, and average other-observer ratings to one another. Where do you see similarities *between categories*?

• Where do you see differences?

• What can you conclude from your findings?

YOUR FEEDBACK FOR
ENCOURAGING THE HEART

Open your feedback report to the two pages on Encouraging the Heart. Review your feedback and answer the questions following the boxed statements. *(Skip questions as necessary if you don't have certain categories of observers.)*

The Six LPI Statements for Encouraging the Heart

5. I praise people for a job well done.

10. I make it a point to let people know about my confidence in their abilities.

15. I make sure that people are creatively rewarded for their contributions to the success of our projects.

20. I publicly recognize people who exemplify commitment to shared values.

25. I find ways to celebrate accomplishments.

30. I give the members of the team lots of appreciation and support for their contributions.

I. Self Ratings

• For which behavior do you have the highest rating?

• The second?

• Third?

• Fourth?

- Fifth?

- Sixth?

- According to your self ratings, which behaviors are your strengths?

- Which behaviors warrant improvement?

2. Average Observer Ratings

- For which behavior did the observers give you the highest rating?

- The second?

- Third?

- Fourth?

- Fifth?

- Sixth?

• Which behaviors do observers indicate are your strengths?

• Which do they indicate are opportunities for improvement?

3. Comparison of Self Ratings to Average Observer Ratings

• What are the similarities?

• What are the differences? What might explain them?

4. Analysis of Individual Observer Ratings

• How does your manager rate you in each of the six behaviors?

• Compare the individual direct reports to one another, the individual coworkers to one another, and the individual other observers to one another. What are the similarities *within each category?*

• What are the differences? What might account for them?

5. Analysis of Ratings and Bar Charts by Categories

• Compare the self, manager, average direct-report, average coworker, and average other-observer ratings to one another. Where do you see similarities *between categories?*

• Where do you see differences?

• What can you conclude from your findings?

CHAPTER 6

Summarizing Your Feedback

By this time you've analyzed a lot of feedback about your use of the five leadership practices that make up the LPI. Take a few minutes now to review your comments in Chapter 5 and summarize them here so that you can make plans for improvement.

At this point you also need to make choices about where to begin. Don't try to work on all of the practices at once; instead, choose one or two that you most want to work on. Then, once you've completed the summary and made your decision, go to Chapter 7 and read the appropriate lists of suggestions on how to improve in the practice(s) you've chosen.

1. What are your strengths, according to your own analysis?

2. What are your strengths, according to the observers?

3. What are your opportunities for improvement, according to your own analysis?

4. What are your opportunities for improvement, according to the observers?

5. What are the areas of greatest agreement between yourself and the observers?

6. What are the areas of greatest disagreement?

7. Where would you most like to focus your efforts in improving your use of the five leadership practices? Rank order the practices in terms of your development priorities.

_____ Challenging the Process

_____ Inspiring a Shared Vision

_____ Enabling Others to Act

_____ Modeling the Way

_____ Encouraging the Heart

8. Which specific behaviors would you most like to work on?

CHAPTER 7

Continuing Your Leadership Development

With the help of the LPI, you've been given the gift of feedback about your leadership practices. And with the help of this workbook, you've taken a hard look at yourself as a leader. Now it's time to act on the insights you've gained. It's time to start becoming an even-better leader than you are today.

THREE OPPORTUNITIES FOR LEARNING TO LEAD

Just how do you learn to lead? We posed that question in our research, and from an analysis of thousands of responses we identified three major opportunities for learning to lead: trial and error, observation, and education.

The purpose of this chapter is to acquaint you with ways to take advantage of these three opportunities. For each of the five practices, we've provided suggestions for all three opportunities. You'll find them under the headings "Learning by Doing," "Learning from Others," and "Learning in the Classroom or on Your Own." But before you proceed to the ideas for the individual practices, we'd like to offer our perspective on the roles of trial and error, observation, and education in leadership development.

Trial and error: Learning by doing. There's no suitable substitute for learning by doing. Whether it's facilitating your team's meetings, leading a special task force, heading your favorite charity's fund-raising drive, or chairing your professional association's annual conference, the more chances you have to serve in leadership roles, the more likely it is that you'll develop the skills to lead—and the more likely that you'll learn the important leadership lessons that come only from the failures and successes of live action.

Just any experience, however, does not by itself support individual development. Challenge is crucial to learning and career enhancement. Boring, routine jobs don't help you improve your skills and abilities. You must stretch. You must take opportunities to test yourself against new and difficult tasks. So experience can indeed be the best teacher—if it includes the element of personal challenge. Whether you choose activities from our "Learning by Doing" lists or you invent your own, make sure that your selections involve a stretch for you.

Observation: Learning from others. Other people are excellent sources of guidance: parents, teachers, neighbors, coaches, counselors, artisans, friends, coworkers, mentors, managers. Think about the people who've given you advice and support, filled you with curiosity, let you watch them while they worked, believed you had promise and inspired you to give your best, offered feedback about your behavior and its impact, and taught you the ropes.

What you continue to learn from these people and others can help you become a better leader. As you think about your continuing leadership development, look around for role models, coaches, and teachers in your organization or community. Don't be shy about asking for their help or about watching them at work.

And even though you can't observe them directly, well-known contemporary or past leaders are also an excellent source of learning. Pick up a couple of biographies and read how these people became esteemed leaders.

Education: Learning in the classroom or on your own. Formal training can improve your chances of success. According to a study by the American Society for Training and Development (ASTD), ". . .people who are trained formally in the workplace have a 30 percent higher productivity rate after one year than people who are not formally trained."[4]

You should be spending *at least fifty hours annually* on your personal and professional development. At Motorola and Solectron, two companies that have received the Malcolm Baldrige National Quality Award, people spend *one hundred hours* per year! In fact, Baldrige Award-winning companies in general spend about twice as much on training as the U.S. average of 1.4 percent of payroll.[5] If you want to have this kind of success, take a cue from these companies.

For each practice you want to improve, commit to participating in at least one formal workshop or seminar during the next few months. Also consider the possibility of self-directed training—a course that you can complete on your own time and at your own pace. And once you've completed the training, make sure you experiment with the new behaviors you learn. In the final analysis, everything about learning to be an effective leader is dependent on the most important source of continual personal improvement: learning by doing.

Now review the developmental priorities that you listed in Chapter 6, and then turn to the appropriate page in this chapter to find ideas about how to improve your leadership ability: Challenging the Process, page 58; Inspiring a Shared Vision, page 62; Enabling Others to Act, page 66; Modeling the Way, page 71; and Encouraging the Heart, page 76.

---

[4]*From* Put Quality to Work: Train America's Workforce *by A.P. Carnevale, Alexandria, VA: American Society for Training and Development, 1990, p. 11. See also* Accounting for United States Economic Growth 1929–1969 *by E. Denison, Washington, DC: The Brookings Institution, 1988.*
[5]*A.P. Carnevale,* Put Quality to Work: Train America's Workforce, *Alexandria, VA: American Society for Training and Development, 1990, p. 11.*

IMPROVING IN CHALLENGING THE PROCESS

Leaders *search for opportunities* to change the status quo. They look for innovative ways to improve their organizations. They *experiment and take risks*. And because risk taking involves mistakes and failure, leaders accept the inevitable disappointments as learning opportunities.

Following are some suggestions on how to improve in Challenging the Process. Put a check mark next to each one that could work for you. Below each idea you choose, write a brief note about a specific action you could take to implement that idea in your particular situation. Feel free to add ideas of your own.

Learning by Doing

____ Volunteer for a tough assignment in your workplace or your community. Be proactive in looking for chances to stretch yourself and learn something.

____ Treat every day as if it were your first day at work. Accept it as a brand-new challenge. Ask yourself "What can I do today so that I'll do my job better and smarter than yesterday?"

____ Make a list of every task you perform. About each, ask yourself "Why am I doing this? Why am I doing it this way? Can this task be eliminated or done significantly better?"

____ Begin your next staff meeting with the following question: "What action did you take last week to make your performance even better this week?" Persist in asking this question for at least three meetings in a row so that everyone knows you're serious about continual improvement. By the way, be prepared to answer this same question for yourself at each meeting.

____ Don't let weekly staff meetings become strictly status reports. Devote at least 25 percent of the time to improving processes and developing new products or services.

_____ About every policy and procedure in your organization or unit, ask "Why are we doing it this way?" If the answer is "Because we've always done it this way," respond with "Well, how is it contributing to making us the best we can be?" If you don't get a satisfactory answer, eliminate or significantly improve the process or procedure so that it does contribute.

_____ Hold a meeting with employees and ask them what really annoys them about the organization or unit. Commit to changing three of the most frequently mentioned items that are hindering success.

_____ Go shopping for ideas. Visit a local business—anything from a restaurant to a machine shop. Don't come back until you see one thing that the business does very well and that your organization could and should copy. Then follow through.

_____ Identify a process in your organization that's broken. Maybe it's your compensation system, maybe it's your sales strategy, or maybe it's your order-fulfillment process. Whatever it is, take action to fix it.

_____ Set up a pilot project for an innovative way of doing something. Maybe it's a new merchandising approach, maybe it's a new intake process, or maybe it's a new software program that will make everyone more effective. Try it on a small scale first. Learn from it. Try some more.

_____ Reward risk takers. Praise them. Give them prizes. Give them the opportunity to talk about their experiences and share the lessons they've learned. It's money in the bank.

_____ Stand up for your beliefs, even if you're a minority of one.

_____ What else can you do to challenge the status quo?

____ What else can you do to experiment with new ways of doing things?

____ What other ways can you find to support people as they seek challenging opportunities and experiment with new ways of doing things?

Learning from Others

____ Identify a couple of successful people in your organization who excel at Challenging the Process. Interview them about what they think are the ingredients for innovation and experimentation. Ask them how they "get away with" challenging the status quo.

____ Identify a couple of successful people in other organizations who excel at Challenging the Process. Interview them, too.

____ Follow a challenger as he or she goes about daily activities. Make notes about what this person does.

____ Read biographies about a couple of revolutionaries in business, science, politics, religion, or any endeavor. Learn whatever you can from the accounts of their lives.

Learning in the Classroom or on Your Own

_____ Read a book from the recommended list for Challenging the Process (see Appendix A).

_____ Take a course in creative problem solving.

_____ Take a course in new-product development.

_____ Take a course in entrepreneurship.

_____ Spend time in an Outward Bound or similar wilderness-adventure program.

_____ Take a class in a subject that you know nothing about. Take notes not only on the content of the course, but also on how it feels to go through the process.

_____ What other courses can you take to experience new things? Which would represent risks for you?

IMPROVING IN INSPIRING A SHARED VISION

Leaders passionately believe that they can make a difference. They *envision the future,* creating ideal and unique images of what the organization can become. Through their magnetism and quiet persuasion, leaders *enlist others* in their dreams. They breathe life into visions and get people to see the exciting possibilities of the future.

Following are some suggestions on how to improve in Inspiring a Shared Vision. Put a check mark next to each one that could work for you. Below each idea you choose, write a brief note about a specific action you could take to implement that idea in your particular situation. Feel free to add ideas of your own.

Learning by Doing

_____ Become a futurist. Join the World Futures Society. Read *American Demographics* or other magazines about future trends. Use the Internet to find a "futures" conference that you can attend. Make a list of what reputable people are predicting will happen in the next ten years. Look for patterns in these trends; figure out how your organization will be affected.

_____ Ask yourself "Am I in the job *to do something* or am I in it *for something to do*?" If your answer is "To do something."—which we assume it will be—then write down what you want to accomplish while you're in your current job and why. Make sure you can answer this question: Five years from now, if you were bragging to someone about what you had accomplished in your current job, what would you say?

_____ Envision yourself ten years from now. Write an article about how you've made a difference in the last decade—how you've contributed to your job, your organization, your family, your community.

_____ Interview some of your key constituents and ask them about their hopes, dreams, goals, and aspirations for the future. How do these relate to your own? How can you incorporate their aspirations into yours?

_____ Meet with your constituents and ask them to share their hopes and dreams with one another. Ask them to listen carefully and identify common goals. Make those common goals visible.

_____ Close your eyes and visualize yourself five years in the future. What will you be doing? What will those you work with be doing? What will your family be doing? What differences will there be in the ways that people work and live? Get as clear a picture as possible.

_____ Turn what you imagine about the future into a five- to ten-minute "vision speech" for your organization. Keep the written speech in your daily planner. Review it daily, revising and refining as you feel moved to do so.

_____ Read your vision speech to someone who will give you constructive feedback. Ask the person these questions: "Is the speech imaginative or conservative? Is it unique or ordinary? Does it evoke visual images? Is it oriented toward the future or toward the present? Does it offer a view that can be shared by others?"

_____ Deliver your vision speech at every opportunity: at team meetings, at company meetings, at club meetings, at home. Publish it and disseminate it widely. Ask people for feedback. Ask them specifically if they could see themselves as part of this future.

_____ Set aside time every week to talk about the future with your staff. Make your vision of the future part of a staff meeting, a working lunch, a conversation by the coffee machine, etc.

_____ Whenever possible, volunteer to stand up in front of a group and speak, even if it's just to introduce someone or make an announcement.

_____ What else can you do to clarify the kind of future you'd like people to create together?

_____ What else can you do to forecast what the future will be like or to scan for future trends? Can you set up an ongoing process?

_____ What else can you do to learn more about your constituents' needs and dreams?

_____ How can you get more input from people on a shared vision?

Learning from Others

_____ Read a biography of a person who's considered to be visionary.

_____ Visit your local library or go to a store that sells CDs, tapes, and videos. Check out or buy and then listen to several famous speeches by leaders who've inspired a shared vision. One example is Martin Luther King's "I Have a Dream" speech. Learn everything you can from the masters.

_____ Watch the C-SPAN channel on television or attend a lecture given by an inspirational speaker. Pick up a few tips on how to express yourself with conviction and enthusiasm. Another good idea is to watch a speaker who's boring and doesn't connect with the audience. Then you can make notes on what *not* to do.

_____ Interview a speech writer. Ask him or her to share methods for constructing an inspirational speech.

_____ Go to a concert or an opera. Observe how the conductor uses his or her body and energy to bring forth the best in others.

Learning in the Classroom or on Your Own

_____ Read a book from the recommended list for Inspiring a Shared Vision (see Appendix A).

_____ Join Toastmasters.

_____ Take a course in giving effective presentations.

_____ Take a course in interpersonal-communication skills.

_____ Take singing lessons.

_____ Take acting lessons.

IMPROVING IN ENABLING OTHERS TO ACT

Leaders *foster collaboration* and build spirited teams. They actively involve others. Leaders understand that mutual respect is what sustains extraordinary efforts; they strive to create an atmosphere of trust and human dignity. They *strengthen others,* making each person feel capable and powerful.

Following are some suggestions on how to improve in Enabling Others to Act. Put a check mark next to each one that could work for you. Below each idea you choose, write a brief note about a specific action you could take to implement that idea in your particular situation. Feel free to add ideas of your own.

Learning by Doing

_____ Find ways to increase interactions among people who need to work more effectively together. Teamwork and trust can only be built when people interact informally as well as formally. Establish easily accessible, common meeting areas that encourage people to interact. Put the coffee pot and popcorn maker in a location between groups that should talk with each other. Ask people from other parts of the organization to attend your regular staff meetings. Schedule a lunch for two groups that don't spend much time face to face.

_____ Treat *every* job as a project. Instead of looking at a job as a linear series of tasks, think of it as a project involving people from a variety of functions. Ask yourself which people should be involved. Call them together at the beginning.

_____ For the next two weeks, commit to replacing the word "I" with "we." As a leader you can't do the job alone; extraordinary things are accomplished as a result of group efforts, not individual efforts. "We" is an inclusive word that signals a commitment to teamwork and sharing. Use it liberally.

_____ Never use the word "subordinate." Use "associate" or "team member."

_____ Volunteer to be the chairperson of a professional, civic, or industry association. Working with volunteers will teach you collaborative skills and give you opportunities to use them.

_____ Assign important tasks to others. For example, if a presentation to a key customer is coming up, ask a promising young staff member to prepare the presentation and deliver it. Coach and support that person.

_____ Assign nonroutine work to people who often do routine work. Routine work breeds a sense of being powerless, whereas nonroutine work fosters a sense of doing something important.

_____ Ask coworkers for their opinions and viewpoints. Share problems with them.

_____ Make sure that everyone in your organization or unit receives at least forty hours of job-related training each year.

_____ Hang out at the coffee machine first thing in the morning. You'll encounter several of your associates. Engage in conversations about how things are going in their lives outside work.

_____ Wander around the plant or office daily. Make sure to stop at everyone's work area and just say "hi."

_____ Keep your door open all of the time, except when you must discuss an extremely private personnel matter. Closed doors send a signal that you don't want to interact with others; they breed distrust and suspicion.

_____ Admit your mistakes. Say "I don't know." Show that you're willing to change your mind when someone comes up with a better idea.

_____ Substantially increase people's signature authority. When people are entrusted to spend the organization's money responsibly, they feel more in control of their own work lives.

_____ Remove unnecessary steps in approval processes.

_____ On a weekly basis, share information about how your unit is doing in terms of meeting its goals. People want to know how things are going. This information makes them feel more powerful.

_____ Ask for volunteers. When you give people a choice about being a part of what's happening, they're much more likely to be committed to a project.

_____ Publicize the work of team members. Shine the spotlight on at least one person each day. At your next staff meeting, tell a story about someone who truly exemplified what teamwork is all about.

_____ What else can you do to enhance people's sense of contribution and self-worth?

_____ What else can you do to make people feel more in control of their own lives?

_____ What else can you do to develop cooperative relationships with your team members or with colleagues in other units?

_____ What else can you do to make yourself more accessible and open to others?

Learning from Others

_____ Hire a professional group facilitator to run several of your meetings and carefully observe how he or she conducts them. Try being a facilitator instead of a manager of meetings.

_____ Hire a personal coach to help you improve in a specific leadership practice or a specific sport. Pay attention to this person's approaches and techniques and then try some of them.

_____ Interview the coach of a professional or amateur athletic team in your area. Ask how you might apply the coach's methods in your organization.

_____ Choose someone in your organization who's known as an exceptional "people person." Accompany and observe this person for a few hours. Ask for tips on how you can do better.

_____ Periodically trade places with employees and do their jobs. This is a terrific way to develop empathy and understanding, which contribute to trust.

Learning in the Classroom or on Your Own

_____ Read a book from the recommended list for Enabling Others to Act (see Appendix A).

_____ Take a course in team building.

_____ Take a course in listening skills.

_____ Take a course on how to run group meetings.

_____ Take a course on consulting skills.

_____ Get on the Internet and join a chat room.

_____ Try out some groupware, such as Lotus Notes® or Novell® GroupWise™.

_____ Study a social movement (e.g., civil rights or women's suffrage) and find out how proponents encouraged others to become involved.

IMPROVING IN MODELING THE WAY

Leaders establish values about how constituents, colleagues, and customers ought to be treated. They create standards of excellence and then *set an example* for others to follow. Because complex change can overwhelm people and stifle action, leaders plan milestones to reach along the way so that others can *achieve small wins*. They unravel bureaucracy, put up signposts, and create opportunities for victory.

Following are some suggestions on how to improve in Modeling the Way. Put a check mark next to each one that could work for you. Below each idea you choose, write a brief note about a specific action you could take to implement that idea in your particular situation. Feel free to add ideas of your own.

Learning by Doing

____ Clarify your personal credo—the values or principles that you believe should guide your part of the organization. Make sure that you communicate your credo orally and in writing to your key constituents. Post it prominently for everyone to see.

____ Ask others on your team to write their credos and share them at one of your team meetings. Ask the members to come to consensus about the values they're prepared to live out in their work. If you have a set of organizational values, compare your team's to the organization's. If there's any incompatibility, resolve it.

____ Keep track of how you spend your time. Check to see whether your actions are consistent with your team's values. If you find inconsistency, figure out what you need to do to align your actions with the values.

____ Learn to say "yes" and "no." For instance, if top quality is your priority, say "no" to every flaw that passes by you. And if you're invited to give a talk on quality, say "yes." Conviction and consistency in saying "yes" and "no" tell people how serious you really are.

_____ Develop a list of questions that you can ask to find out whether your team members are living out the team's values. Ask these questions at staff meetings. For example, ask people what they've done in the last week to make sure their work is top quality.

_____ Include values in performance appraisals. Make sure that you and others are evaluated according to how well you live out your values.

_____ Be expressive—even emotional—about your beliefs. If you're proud of your people for living up to high performance standards, let them know. Then go brag about them to others. Tell stories about people who are living out values in memorable ways.

_____ Keep your daily planner at hand. Write down your promises as you make them. Make sure that you review them daily and fulfill them on schedule. Also be sure to let others know that you've done what you said you'd do.

_____ Do something dramatic to demonstrate your commitment to a team value. For instance, if creativity is a value, take everyone to a local toy store, buy a few kids' games, and spend a couple of hours playing them. Then spend an hour discussing what people learned about creativity that could be applied to their own work or to the organization.

_____ Set goals that are achievable. Tell people what the key milestones are so that they can easily see their progress.

_____ Focus on the little things—not just the big ones—so that people know you value the quality of their work lives. Fixing a leaky roof is just as important as constructing a beautiful new building. What "leaky roofs" are there around your organization, and what can you do to fix them?

_____ Make decisions visible. Use a centrally located bulletin board to post reminders of the team's decisions. Keep the board updated with information on progress.

_____ Set a personal example for others by behaving in ways that demonstrate and reinforce your stated values. If collaboration is a value in your organization, for example, make sure that you act as a team player.

_____ What else can you do to clarify your own and others' values?

_____ What else can you do to communicate and build consensus around values?

_____ In what other ways can you pay attention to and personally set an example of your team's values?

_____ What else can you do to set clear goals, make plans, and establish milestones for the projects you lead?

Learning from Others

____ Watch the film *Gandhi* with some colleagues. Afterward, discuss how Gandhi set an example for his constituents.

____ Choose some other famous leader that you consider to be a role model. Learn whatever you can from that person by reading a biography or watching a film about him or her.

____ Ask several trusted colleagues to choose the two or three most credible people in your organization. Interview these people. Spend time with them.

____ Pay attention to what people say is important to them. Then look for actions that are examples of living out their values. Look for contradictions as well. Keep in mind that others are paying attention to whether your words and deeds are consistent!

____ Visit a retail store that's widely acknowledged for its extraordinary customer service. Watch and listen to what the store employees do and say. Shop there and see how you're treated. Interview a couple of the employees about how the store got such a stellar reputation.

____ Spend some time with someone you personally look to as a role model. Ask that person for advice on how to make behavior consistent with values.

Learning in the Classroom or on Your Own

_____ Read a book from the recommended list for Modeling the Way (see Appendix A).

_____ Take a group or self-directed course in clarifying personal values.

_____ Take a course in time management, especially one in which you're asked to keep track of how you spend your time, and then check your activities for consistency with your values.

_____ Take a story-telling class. Practice telling stories every time you get the opportunity.

_____ Take a course in goal setting and action planning.

_____ Purchase and use software for contact management and personal productivity. This software can assist you in automating some of your time-management processes.

_____ Buy and use a software program for performance appraisal.

IMPROVING IN ENCOURAGING THE HEART

Getting extraordinary things done in organizations is hard work. To keep hope and determination alive, leaders *recognize contributions* that individuals make in the climb to the top. And because the members of every winning team need to share in the rewards of their efforts, leaders *celebrate accomplishments*. They make people feel like heroes.

Following are some suggestions on how to improve in Encouraging the Heart. Put a check mark next to each one that could work for you. Below each idea you choose, write a brief note about a specific action you could take to implement that idea in your particular situation. Feel free to add ideas of your own.

Learning by Doing

____ Wander around your office area for the express purpose of finding someone in the act of doing something that exemplifies the organization's standards. Find a way to recognize that person on the spot.

____ Reward first those who perform above the stated expectations. Ask yourself which of your constituents best embodies the team's values and priorities. Think of three ways to single out (praise and reward) that person in the weeks to come.

____ If you have annual bonuses, link a portion of them to the extent to which people model the values expected.

____ Plan a festive celebration for each small milestone that your team reaches. Don't wait until the whole project is finished to celebrate.

____ Tell a public story about a person in your organization who went above and beyond the call of duty.

____ Involve others in designing reward and recognition systems. The resulting systems are more likely to link rewards to performance.

_____ Give people tools that they can use to recognize one another, such as index cards or notepads printed with the message "You Made My Day." Create a culture in which peers recognize peers.

_____ Make creative use of rewards. Use your imagination and have some fun. Give a giant light bulb to the person who has the best idea of the month—or chocolate candy to the person who makes the office run "sweetly." Tailor ideas to your own team.

_____ Say "thank you" when you appreciate something that someone has done.

_____ Write at least three thank-you notes each day. We've never heard anyone complain about being thanked too much, but we've heard lots of complaints about being thanked too little!

_____ Provide feedback about results, and the sooner the better. Feedback can range from a simple "well done" to a detailed debriefing session on how the latest project went and what the team members learned.

_____ Be personally involved. If you don't attend staff celebrations and parties, you're sending the message that you're not interested.

_____ Set aside one day each year as a special organizational-celebration day, much like Independence Day or Mardi Gras.

_____ Create your organization's "Hall of Fame"—an area that recognizes all the people who've done extraordinary things.

_____ Put on a clown costume or some other funny outfit and walk around the office distributing balloons. This may sound silly, but it will be noticed, you'll have fun, and it will liven up the place.

____ What else can you do to recognize and reward individual contributions?

____ What else can you do to celebrate team accomplishments?

Learning from Others

____ Go to a local athletic event. Watch the cheerleaders and the players as they celebrate small wins and big victories. Learn what you can from them about enthusiasm and passion.

____ Ask for advice and coaching from someone you know who's much better at Encouraging the Heart than you are.

____ Ask people how they would like to be recognized for their accomplishments or successes.

____ Attend an award ceremony for someone in your community or organization and make notes on what you like about it. Try some of the same methods the next time you hold an award ceremony.

_____ When you're at a wedding or holiday celebration, make notes on what you like about the celebration. Apply these ideas to your situation.

_____ Talk to people in your organization who have a reputation for helping others to develop. Ask them how they encourage others to excel.

_____ Sit on a bench in a local park and watch children play. Observe how they encourage one another.

Learning in the Classroom or on Your Own

_____ Read a book from the recommended list for Encouraging the Heart (see Appendix A).

_____ Take an improvisational-theater class.

_____ Take a class on creativity.

_____ Take a course in drawing, painting, or photography.

_____ Learn to use a software program that creates graphics.

_____ Take an advertising course.

CHAPTER 8

Making Action Plans

On the next two pages are two action-planning forms. Complete one form for each leadership practice in which you want to improve. (Remember that you shouldn't work on more than two practices at one time.)

Before you start filling out these forms, we recommend that you make several copies in case you need more than one sheet for one practice. Also, several months from now, you may find that you want to make new action plans to improve in other practices.

The form asks you to make decisions about:

- Your improvement goal (the specific objective you want to accomplish)

- Action items (the specific steps you'll take to meet your improvement goal)

- Measures of success (the evidence that will indicate you've succeeded)

- Completion dates (the dates by which you will have completed the action items and achieved your goal)

- Support (someone to whom you can turn for coaching, advice, and encouragement)

ACTION-PLANNING FORM

Leadership Practice	Improvement Goal	Action Items	Measures of Success	Completion Dates	Support

ACTION-PLANNING FORM

Leadership Practice	Improvement Goal	Action Items	Measures of Success	Completion Dates	Support

CHAPTER 9

Discussing Your LPI Feedback with Others

In completing the LPI process, you asked others to give you the gift of feedback about your leadership practices. When people offer feedback, they like to know whether you value this gift, whether it was useful, and what you intend to do with it.

By sharing your LPI feedback, you can tell people what they need to know and, at the same time, put all of the five practices to work for you:

Challenging the Process. Openly discussing your own leadership behavior may be something entirely new for you. It may even be unprecedented in your organization. Whether it's a new experience or not, it certainly gives you a chance to take a risk and make yourself vulnerable.

Inspiring a Shared Vision. When you share your feedback, you have a chance to talk about your hopes and dreams for the future as you improve your leadership abilities.

Enabling Others to Act. Sharing your feedback says "I trust you with this information about me. All of us belong to this team, and we're all trying to improve together. I can't do it alone."

Modeling the Way. Sharing your feedback sets the kind of example you'd like others to follow: being open about information that's relevant to improving the team. You are living the values of honesty, trust, and teamwork.

Encouraging the Heart. When you genuinely thank people for giving you feedback, you recognize their contributions. You can also thank them by providing coffee, juice, and muffins!

So we encourage you to share your feedback with those who gave you this gift. And we encourage you to use this sharing as a way to improve further in each of the leadership practices.

SHARING IN A GROUP OR IN ONE-ON-ONE SESSIONS

Either you can invite all those who gave you feedback to a group meeting, or you can schedule a one-on-one meeting with each of them. In deciding which alternative to choose, consider your own comfort level, the norms of your organization, and the comfort level of those who gave you the feedback.

Feedback meetings can be tough, but they can also benefit both you and your constituents. Just the fact that you're making the effort to share your LPI feedback will mean a lot to people.

GUIDELINES FOR THE FEEDBACK MEETING

Following these guidelines will increase your chances of having a meeting that's beneficial to everyone:

1. Prepare yourself. Develop an agenda so that you can keep the meeting focused and on track. Plan what you want to say and how you want to say it. Plan how you'll inform people and involve them. Refer to your action plan(s) so that you can include specific information about what you're going to do as a result of the feedback. If you need help, ask a consultant or human resources person to coach you ahead of time or attend the feedback meeting.

2. Schedule the meeting. It's best to share feedback in an organized fashion, so set up the group meeting or the individual sessions ahead of time.

3. Protect anonymity. The people who gave you feedback assumed that their individual scores would remain anonymous. The only exception is your manager, if he or she completed an LPI-Observer form. So under no circumstances should you ask people to disclose who gave you which scores. Nor should people be pressured by others to disclose, which means that you must intervene if this happens. If people volunteer their scores, that's another matter; then it's their choice.

4. Express your gratitude. Begin the discussion by saying "thank you." Let people know that you appreciate their feedback and their willingness to talk with you further about it. Make people feel comfortable.

5. Set ground rules. At the beginning of the meeting, establish a few ground rules. Let people know how the meeting will run, how long it will take, and what will be discussed. Also let them know what you expect from them, such as further information about specific things that you can do more of or less of (review your notes in Chapter 5 about additional information you needed). Finally, establish some rules about dealing with feedback during the meeting. (See "Ground Rules for Feedback" in this chapter.)

6. Describe the leadership model. Give a brief overview of the five practices. The descriptions in Chapters 2 and 7 can be used for this purpose.

7. Express your feelings. Let people know how you feel about the feedback you received. By expressing your feelings, you will more easily establish trust and rapport.

8. Show your scores. If you're sharing your actual scores (and we highly recommend that you do), either display them on overhead transparencies or distribute copies. If you choose not to show the scores, you may summarize them orally.

9. Talk about strengths (highest scores). Start with what you do well, according to the observers. Cite specific examples: "My highest ratings were in the practice of Enabling Others to Act. I think I demonstrated this practice when I asked Leslie and Tom to give the annual report to the department heads instead of giving it myself. That's an example of Enabling." Ask people to share their own specific examples of how you've demonstrated the practice. Then ask them how you can become even better.

10. Talk about opportunities for improvement (lowest scores). Define your understanding and perception of the feedback. Cite examples of instances in which you may not have done as well as you could. Ask others for specific examples. Then get feedback on how you can improve.

11. Discuss the practice that shows the largest gap between your LPI-Self and LPI-Observer scores. Ask people to help you understand why there's such a difference between your perceptions of yourself and their perceptions of you. For example, you might ask "What do I do that contributes to being misunderstood?" or "What am I missing? Is there something I do that accounts for this difference in perception?"

12. Ask for any other feedback and suggestions. Encourage people to contribute their ideas. You need their help if you and they are to be effective together.

13. Share your action plan(s). Tell people specifically what you plan to do over the next several weeks to improve. Ask them to hold you accountable and to give you positive reinforcement when they see that you're doing what you said you would do. (It's important that you get positive reinforcement along the way.) Let people know that you probably won't get new behaviors entirely right the first time, but that you'll keep trying and learning.

14. Encourage people to get feedback on their own leadership practices. Express your appreciation to them for their willingness to give you feedback and to participate in the discussion of your LPI results. Then encourage them to do the same with their own constituents. Now that they've seen how helpful feedback can be, urge them to take advantage of the same process. Explain that it doesn't matter whether they're managers or not: Everyone has to function as a leader at some point, and everyone can benefit from learning how to be a better leader.[6]

Ground Rules for Feedback

In general, you'll need to pay special attention to the rules for receiving feedback, and your constituents will need to pay special attention to the rules for giving feedback. However, it's a good idea to discuss the rules for both giving and receiving feedback, because these activities represent essential team skills that you and your constituents need to develop in order to work together effectively.

In addition to explaining these rules, you should post a copy of them prominently. If you want, you may distribute individual copies as well.

Rules for Giving Feedback

1. Acknowledge aloud that it's tough to give honest feedback.

2. Avoid personal attacks.

3. Focus on specific behaviors—not attitudes, characterizations, or personalities. For example, say "When you cut me off in last week's meeting, I felt powerless" instead of "You're really rude."

4. Connect behaviors to results. For example, say "When you don't follow through on your commitment to be at meetings on time, I get behind in my own work and have to work overtime to catch up. That makes me less efficient in my work."

5. Avoid hearsay, accusations, and exaggerations. Relate only what you have personally experienced. Let others speak for themselves.

---

[6]*Kouzes and Posner have developed a version of the LPI for those leaders not in management positions who want to improve their use of The Five Practices—The Leadership Practices Inventory—Individual Contributor (LPI-IC), available from Jossey-Bass/Pfeiffer.*

6. Provide information that's constructive: "If you had acknowledged that you received those improvement ideas I left in your in-basket, I would have felt that I was being listened to."

7. Include positive as well as negative feedback. People need to know what they're doing well in order to believe that they can improve. They also need to know what success looks like in order to have goals.

Rules for Receiving Feedback

1. Acknowledge aloud that it's tough to receive feedback.

2. Approach feedback as a *partnership process,* not a debate.

3. Focus energy on understanding the behavior being discussed, not fixing it right then and there. You might need time to consider alternatives, gather more information, check facts, and so on.

4. Don't be reluctant to ask questions to gain a better understanding of the feedback. Request specific examples so that you'll know which behaviors people are referring to.

5. Confirm your understanding: "If I understand correctly, you're saying. . . ."

6. Take feedback seriously. Bring a notepad and take notes.

7. Seek a balance between positive and negative feedback. If you receive only positive feedback, ask about practices or behaviors in which you could improve. If you receive only negative feedback, ask about practices or behaviors in which you're strong.

APPENDIX A

Recommended Readings

CHALLENGING THE PROCESS

Calvert, G. (1993). *Highwire management: Risk-taking tactics for leaders, innovators, and trailblazers.* San Francisco: Jossey-Bass.

Csikszentmihalyi, M. (1990). *Flow: The psychology of optimal experience.* New York: HarperCollins.

Jaffe, D.T., Scott, C.D., & Tobe, G.R. (1994). *Rekindling commitment: How to revitalize yourself, your work, and your organization.* San Francisco: Jossey-Bass.

Kanter, R.M. (1983). *The change masters: Innovation for productivity in the American corporation.* New York: Simon & Schuster.

Kriegel, R., & Patler, L. (1991). *If it ain't broke...break it!* New York: Warner.

Peters, T. (1992). *Liberation management: Necessary disorganization for the nanosecond nineties.* New York: Knopf.

INSPIRING A SHARED VISION

Bennis, W., & Nanus, B. (1985). *Leaders: The strategies for taking charge.* New York: HarperCollins.

Hamel, G., & Prahalad, C.K. (1994). *Competing for the future: Breakthrough strategies for seizing control of your industry and creating the markets of tomorrow.* Boston: Harvard Business School Press.

Nanus, B. (1992). *Visionary leadership: Creating a compelling sense of direction for your organization.* San Francisco: Jossey-Bass.

Pearce, T. (1995). *Leading out loud.* San Francisco: Jossey-Bass.

Peck, M.S. (1978). *The road less traveled.* New York: Simon & Schuster.

Quigley, J.V. (1993). *Vision: How leaders develop it, share it and sustain it.* New York: McGraw-Hill.

Schwartz, F. (1991). *The art of the long view.* New York: Currency.

Wheatley, M. (1992). *Leadership and the new science,* Second Edition. San Francisco: Berrett-Koehler.

ENABLING OTHERS TO ACT

Block, P. (1987). *The empowered manager: Positive political skills at work.* San Francisco: Jossey-Bass.

Case, J. (1995). *Open-book management: The coming business revolution.* New York: HarperCollins.

Fisher, R., & Ury, W. (1981). *Getting to yes.* Boston: Houghton Mifflin.

Hakim, C. (1994). *We are all self-employed.* San Francisco: Berrett-Koehler.

Helgesen, S. (1995). *The web of inclusion.* New York: Currency.

Lawler, E.E., III. (1992). *The ultimate advantage: Creating the high-involvement organization.* San Francisco: Jossey-Bass.

Pfeffer, J. (1994). *Competitive advantage through people: Unleashing the power of the work force.* Boston: Harvard Business School Press.

Stack, J. (1992). *The great game of business: The only sensible way to run a company.* New York: Currency.

Tannen, D. (1994). *Talking from 9 to 5: How women's and men's conversational styles affect who gets heard, who gets credit, and what gets done at work.* New York: William Morrow.

Wellins, R.E., Byham, W.C., & Wilson, J.M. (1991). *Empowered teams: Creating self-directed work groups that improve quality, productivity, and participation.* San Francisco: Jossey-Bass.

MODELING THE WAY

Armstrong, D. (1992). *Managing by storying around: A new method of leadership.* New York: Currency.

Collins, J., & Porras, J. (1994). *Built to last: Successful habits of visionary companies.* New York: HarperCollins.

DePree, M. (1989). *Leadership is an art.* New York: Doubleday.

DePree, M. (1992). *Leadership jazz.* New York: Doubleday.

Kouzes, J.M., & Posner, B.Z. (1993). *Credibility: How leaders gain and lose it, why people demand it.* San Francisco: Jossey-Bass.

Schwarzkopf, H.N., with Pietre, P. (1992). *It doesn't take a hero.* New York: Bantam.

ENCOURAGING THE HEART

Deal, T.E., & Jenkins, W.A. (1994). *Managing the hidden organization: Strategies for empowering your behind-the-scenes employees.* New York: Warner.

Kohn, A. (1993). *Punished by rewards.* New York: Houghton Mifflin.

Nelson, B. (1994). *1001 ways to reward employees.* New York: Workman.

Peterson, C., & Bossio, L.M. (1991). *Health and optimism: New research on the relationship between positive thinking and physical well-being.* New York: Free Press.

Seligman, M. (1990). *Learned optimism.* New York: Knopf.

Vroom, V.H. (1994). *Work and motivation.* San Francisco: Jossey-Bass.

OTHER BOOKS ON LEADERSHIP

Bennis, W. (1989). *On becoming a leader.* Reading, MA: Addison-Wesley.

Bass, B.M., & Stodgill, R.M. (1990). *Bass & Stodgill's handbook of leadership.* New York: Free Press.

Gardner, H. (1995). *Leading minds.* New York: HarperCollins.

Gardner, J. (1989). *On leadership.* New York: Free Press.

Heifetz, R.A. (1994). *Leadership without easy answers.* Cambridge, MA: Belknap.

Peters, T., & Austin, N. (1983). *A passion for excellence: The leadership difference.* New York: Random House.

APPENDIX B

Instructions for Hand Scoring[7]

On the following pages are five grids (one for each practice) that you can use to record your LPI scores. The first grid, which is for Challenging the Process, asks you to record scores for LPI items 1, 6, 11, 16, 21, and 26. These are the items that relate to behaviors involved in Challenging the Process. An abbreviated form of each item is printed beside the grid as a handy reference. Each of the remaining four grids is constructed in the same way, listing abbreviations of the LPI items that pertain to that practice.

To record your LPI-Self and LPI-Observer scores for each practice, transfer the numbers from the response sheets to the scoring grid. Under the heading "Self Rating," record the scores that you gave yourself.

Under the heading "Observers' Ratings" you'll notice that there are enough columns to accommodate twenty observers. Record each observer's ratings in one of the columns.

If you have separate observer categories, fill in the blanks for *observer column headings* with "M" for your manager's scores, "D1" for the first direct report whose scores you record, "D2" for the second direct report, "C1" for the first coworker, "C2" for the second coworker, and so on. If you don't have observer categories, fill in the column headings with "O1," "O2," and so on for other observers.

After you've recorded all scores for Challenging the Process, total each column and write the sums in the row marked "Totals." Transfer your self total to the blank marked "Self Total." Then add all of the observers' totals. (Don't include the self total.) Write this grand total in the blank marked "Total of All Observers' Scores." To obtain the average observer score, divide the grand total by the number of observers. Then write this average in the blank marked "Observer Average." Figure 8 shows how the grid would look if scores for self and five observers had been entered.

After you've filled in the grids, it's a good idea to make copies of them so that you can place the copies next to the pages in Chapter 5 and refer to your scores easily as you analyze your feedback.

---

[7]*If your LPI-Self and LPI-Observer forms are being computer scored, ignore this appendix.*

CHALLENGING THE PROCESS

	SELF RATING	OBSERVERS' RATINGS							
		M	D₁	D₂	C₁	C₂			Total of All Observers' Scores
1. Seeks challenging opportunities	5	4	2	5	4	1			
6. Challenges people to try new approaches	4	4	3	4	4	2			
11. Looks outside organization for ways to improve	3	3	5	1	1	1			
16. Asks "What can we learn?"	4	2	1	1	5	3			
21. Experiments and takes risks	2	5	2	3	2	5			
26. Takes initiative to overcome obstacles	5	1	3	2	3	2			
TOTALS	23	19	16	16	19	14			84

Self Total: 23

Observer Average: 16.8

FIGURE 8. Sample Completed Grid

CHALLENGING THE PROCESS

	SELF RATING	OBSERVERS' RATINGS	Total of All Observers' Scores
1. Seeks challenging opportunities	9		
6. Challenges people to try new approaches	9		
11. Looks outside organization for ways to improve	10		
16. Asks "What can we learn?"	10		
21. Experiments and takes risks	9		
26. Takes initiative to overcome obstacles	9		
TOTALS	56		

Self Total: _____

Observer Average: _____

INSPIRING A SHARED VISION

	SELF RATING	OBSERVERS' RATINGS							Total of All Observers' Scores
2. Talks about future trends	9								
7. Describes compelling image of future	9								
12. Appeals to others to share dream of future	10								
17. Shows others how their interests can be realized	8								
22. Is enthusiastic and positive about future	10								
27. Speaks with conviction about meaning of work	10								
TOTALS	56								

Self Total: _____

Observer Average: _____

ENABLING OTHERS TO ACT

	SELF RATING	OBSERVERS' RATINGS																		Total of All Observers' Scores
3. Develops cooperative relationships	10																			
8. Listens to diverse points of view	10																			
13. Treats people with dignity and respect	9																			
18. Supports other people's decisions	9																			
23. Lets people choose how to do their work	10																			
28. Ensures that people grow in their jobs	10																			
TOTALS	58																			

Self Total: _____

Observer Average: _____

MODELING THE WAY

	SELF RATING	OBSERVERS' RATINGS																			Total of All Observers' Scores
4. Sets example of what is expected	8																				
9. Ensures that people adhere to agreed-on standards	6																				
14. Follows through on promises and commitments	8																				
19. Is clear about his/her philosophy of leadership	10																				
24. Ensures that goals, plans, milestones are set	10																				
29. Makes progress toward goals one step at a time	9																				
TOTALS	27																				

Self Total: _____   Observer Average: _____

ENCOURAGING THE HEART

	SELF RATING	OBSERVERS' RATINGS																			Total of All Observers' Scores
5. Praises people for a job well done	8																				
10. Expresses confidence in people's abilities	9																				
15. Creatively rewards people for their contributions	9																				
20. Recognizes people for commitment to shared values	9																				
25. Finds ways to celebrate accomplishments	8																				
30. Gives team members appreciation and support	10																				
TOTALS	53																				

Self Total: _____

Observer Average: _____

PERCENTILE RANKINGS FOR LPI RATINGS

The chart on the opposite page represents the percentile rankings for more than 18,000 of the respondents in Kouzes and Posner's database. This ranking is determined by the percentage of people who score at or below a given number. For example, if your score for "challenging" is at the 70th percentile line on the chart, this means that you scored higher than 70 percent of all the people who have taken the LPI. You would be in the top 30 percent on that dimension.

Put an "S" through the number in each column that corresponds to the number of your LPI-Self Total score on that practice. Connect these five "S"s with a heavy line. Put an "O" through the number in each column that corresponds to the "LPI-Observer Average" for each practice. (While you may have separate observer categories, we recommend, for visual clarity, plotting only the Observer Average, obtained by dividing the total of all observers' scores by the number of observers.) Connect the 5 "O"s with a dotted line. This will give you a graphic representation of your LPI percentile ranking, illustrating the relationship between your self perception and the observations of other people.

Our studies indicate that a "high" score is one at the 70th percentile or above. A "low" score is one at the 30th percentile or below. A score that falls between those ranges would be considered a "moderate" score.

As you look at the graph of your LPI scores—and those from the LPI-Observers—consider where they agree and disagree. Do the lines follow each other in a parallel fashion?

LPI PERCENTILE RANKINGS

Percentile	Challenging	Inspiring	Enabling	Modeling	Encouraging
100	60	60	60	60	60
	59	59			
	58	58	59		
	57		58	59	59
		57			
	56	56		58	58
	55	55	57		57
		54		57	
90	54		56	56	55
		53			
	53				
		52	55	55	54
	52				
		51		54	
80	51	50	54		53
				53	52
	50	49	53		51
		48			
70	49				50
		47	52		
	48			51	49
		46	51		
60	47	45		50	48
	46	44	50	49	47
		43	49		46
50	45	42		48	45
	44	41	48	47	44
	43		47	46	43
40		40			
	42	39	46	45	42
	41	38	45		41
30	40	37		44	40
	39	36	44	43	39
		35		42	38
	38	34	43		37
20	37	33	42	41	36
		32			35
	36	31	41	40	34
	35	30	40	39	33
	34	29	39	38	32
	33	28	38	37	31
10	32	27	37	36	30
	31	26	36	35	29
	30	25	34 35	34	28
	29	24	33	32 33	26 27
	27 28	23	32	31	25
	25	21 22	30 31	29 30	23 24
	23 24	20	27 28 29	27 28	20 21 22
	19 20 21 22	18 19	23 24 25 26	23 24 25 26	17 18 19
1	12 13 14 15 16 17 18	15 16 17	16 17 18 19 20 21 22	16 17 18 19 20 21 22	11 12 13 14 15 16
		10 11 12 13 14			

APPENDIX C

Psychometric Properties of the LPI

RELIABILITY

Reliability refers to the extent to which an instrument contains "measurement errors" that cause scores to differ for reasons unrelated to the respondent: The fewer errors contained, the more reliable the instrument.

Reliability is determined empirically in several ways. One is to split the responses in half and test to see whether the two halves are correlated. If the two halves were completed by the same person at the same time, we would expect the responses from the first half to be reasonably consistent with the responses from the second half. If the two halves were perfectly independent (for example, one-half of an apple and one-half of an orange), we would expect no correlation—although there might be some correlation, given that both items are fruits rather than one fruit and one vegetable. If the halves were perfectly correlated (for example, two halves of the same apple), we would expect a 1.0 correlation coefficient. Statisticians refer to this correlation as *internal reliability.* "Acceptable" internal reliability coefficients are usually .50+. The LPI scales are generally above .80, so we can say that the LPI has strong internal reliability.

Another empirical measure of reliability is called *test-retest reliability,* which has to do with the extent to which an instrument is sensitive to extraneous factors that might affect a respondent's scores from one administration to another: The less sensitive the instrument, the higher its test-retest reliability. For example, time of day, weather, individual personality, political or social events, activity within the organization, and similar factors might affect a respondent's scores from one administration to another. Over periods as short as one or two days and as long as three to four weeks, scores on the LPI show significant test-retest reliability (or consistency) at levels greater than .90 correlation. However, LPI scores would be expected to change from one administration to another if, in the intervening period, respondents attended a leadership workshop such as the one described in this guide, consciously worked on changing their leadership behavior, or experienced significant emotional events at work or in their personal lives.

Finally, reliability is enhanced when an instrument asks about a behavior more than once. This means that a two-item scale is inherently more reliable than a one-item scale, a three-item scale is more reliable than a two-item scale, and so on. The LPI scales contain six items or statements for each of the five key leadership practices.

VALIDITY

Validity has to do with whether an instrument truly measures what it is supposed to measure and whether its scores have meaning for a respondent. Like reliability, validity is determined in several ways.

The most common assessment of validity is called *face validity,* which concerns whether, on the basis of subjective evaluation, an instrument "appears" to be measuring what it is supposed to measure. Given that the items on the LPI are related to the statements that workshop participants generally make about their own or others' personal-best leadership experiences, the LPI has excellent face validity.

Validity is also determined empirically. Factor analysis is used to determine the extent to which the instrument items measure common or different content areas. The results of these analyses consistently reveal that the LPI contains five factors, the items within each factor relating more to one another than to the other factors. For example, the items that measure Challenging the Process are all more related to one another than they are to any of the items measuring the other four practices.

The question of whether the scores have payoff for a respondent is probably a workshop participant's most important concern. To answer this question, we look at determining predictive and/or concurrent validity. In other words, we assess the extent to which LPI scores are associated with other important variables. The LPI has excellent payoff validity, as shown by studies of the relationship between LPI scores and such variables as work-group performance, team cohesiveness, member commitment and loyalty, satisfaction (both with the job and with the leader), upward influence, and credibility.

ABSTRACTS OF LPI THESES, DISSERTATIONS, PAPERS

The LPI has been the subject of many research studies. The rest of this appendix presents abstracts of some of the theses, dissertations, and other papers involving the LPI. Reading it or skimming it for highlights will give you information that you'll find helpful in providing participants with examples of the connection between the LPI behaviors and successful leadership. Check *TheLeadershipChallenge.com* for periodic updates of the normative database and new LPI research findings.

Development of a Modified Version of the Leadership Practices Inventory for Use with College Students

Barbara Brodsky
School of Education
San Jose State University
San Jose, California
Master's Thesis: June 1988

Objective. To create a leadership-development instrument for use with college students and, in the process, to identify the practices or behaviors most frequently used by college students in leadership positions.

Methodology. From "Leadership America" nominees at a small, private, liberal-arts college, 4 students were selected (randomly by gender and upper-division class year) for qualitative case studies and structured interviews about "personal-best experiences as a college student leader." A pilot version of the *Student-LPI,* adapted for terminology and college-student context, was developed and tested with members of the college's "Student Senate." Seventy-nine percent voluntarily participated (7 men and 12 women, equally divided by class year). Each statement was discussed in order to identify items that were difficult to understand, ambiguous, or not applicable. The feedback from this activity was used to further modify the pilot *Student-LPI.*

Key findings. Generally, the inventory statements reflected student leadership behavior. Twenty-five were found to be clear, easy to understand, and composed of terminology that reflected the experiences of student leaders. The remaining 5 were deemed to be problematic (difficult to understand or objectionable).

It was recommended that the pilot *Student-LPI* be further modified in order to be considered an accurate measure of student leadership behavior. In addition, it was recommended that a larger sample group complete the inventory. Overall, the *Student-LPI* was seen as having good potential for use with college students and in leadership-development activities with this population.

Identifying and Analyzing the Practices Utilized by Coaches in Achieving Their "Personal Best" in Coaching

Russell Dean Elliott
Professional Studies (Educational Administration)
Iowa State University
Ames, Iowa
Master's Thesis: June 1990

Objective. To learn more about coaches as leaders and to discover which leadership practices head football coaches use when they are at their personal best.

Methodology. One hundred and ninety-five NCAA Division I head football coaches were asked to complete a 47-item survey concerning their personal-best leadership experiences as coaches. This survey was modified from Kouzes and Posner's *Personal-Best Leadership Experience*. Of the 27 (14 percent) who responded, the majority had held the position of head coach for 1 to 5 years at their present schools, and 15 had been assistant coaches for more than 10 years. Sixteen were Division I-A coaches, and 11 were Division I-AA coaches. All responses were content analyzed by the researcher, based on a coding scheme formed after reviewing the first several returns.

Key findings. Common practices were evident. Ninety-three percent (N = 25) of the coaches' personal-best leadership experiences involved changing existing ways of doing things (Challenging the Process). The need to have a vision and then communicate it (Inspiring a Shared Vision) was mentioned by 22 of the coaches (81 percent). Empowering assistant coaches and "anyone else they can involve in the program" (Enabling Others to Act) was a component of the personal-best experiences of 20 coaches (74 percent). Leading by example and matching actions with values (Modeling the Way) was expressed by all of the coaches (100 percent). Finally, 21 coaches (78 percent) felt the need to recognize achievements and celebrate accomplishments (Encouraging the Heart).

Closer examination of the responses suggested that "communicating the vision and inspiring others to that vision were vitally important for coaches while they achieved their personal best" (p. 32). Elliott concludes that "a competitive edge may be gained by successfully communicating the vision and inspiring others" (p. 32).

The BIA/Contract School Administrator: Implications for At-Risk Native American Students

Edward W. Chance
Department of Educational Leadership and Policy
College of Education
University of Oklahoma
Norman, Oklahoma
Presented at the National Rural and Small School Consortium Meeting, 1990

Objective. To investigate the type of leadership exhibited by secondary school administrators in Bureau of Indian Affairs/Contract schools (the primary educational delivery system for Native Americans residing on reservations).

Methodology. Surveys were sent to 54 secondary school administrators identified in the *Education Directory of the Office of Indian Education Programs.* Twenty-two usable LPI-Self responses were received (41-percent response rate). Most respondents were men (80 percent). About two-fifths (38.5 percent) were Native Americans. Except for ethnicity and degrees of experience, few demographic differences were found between the Native American and non-Native

American school administrators. The majority in both groups identified instructional leadership as their primary job and indicated very similar activities in the daily operation of their schools.

Key findings. The findings suggested that the principals responded to the desire to be instructional leaders but acted, instead, primarily as managers. Only 13 percent were in classes on a daily basis; 17 percent were not in classes even on a monthly basis.

No statistically significant differences in LPI scores were found between Native American administrators and their non-Native American counterparts. Compared to the normative sample, both groups scored relatively high (70th percentile) on Inspiring a Shared Vision and Modeling the Way. The Native American administrators scored above the 70th percentile on Challenging the Process. Both groups scored in the moderate range in Enabling Others to Act and Encouraging the Heart.

Chance concludes, "The administrators perceived an ability to inspire and model, and for one group to challenge, yet failed to enable their subordinates and sufficiently recognize them when they achieved. In other words, both the LPI and the demographic questionnaire indicated an ability to 'talk the talk' but a functional failure in 'walking the talk'."

A Comparison of the Perceptions of School-Based and Centralized-Management Administrators and Teachers Toward Leadership Practices

Ann Nnennaya Okorie
School of Education
Baylor University
Waco, Texas
Doctoral Dissertation: December 1990

Objective. To determine whether significant differences in leadership practices exist between administrators and teachers in school-based districts and administrators and teachers in centrally managed districts.

Methodology. The sample was drawn from 457 public elementary and secondary schools in 4 randomly selected states (South Carolina, Mississippi, Wisconsin, and Michigan). There were 118 administrators and teachers from school-based districts and 114 administrators and teachers from districts with centralized management. The overall survey response rate was 29 percent; 44 percent of the responses were from administrators. The LPI was modified so that respondents marked the frequency with which they believed that each of the leadership behaviors was being practiced "on the campus."

Key findings. There were significant differences between the leadership practices associated with school-based districts and those associated with centrally managed districts. For all five leadership practices, the perceptions of teachers were significantly different from those of administrators. Significant differences were found between teachers and administrators in school-based districts and especially between teachers and administrators in centrally managed districts. (Teachers' perceptions were consistently lower than the views of administrators.) Perceptions about the frequency of leadership actions and behaviors were consistently higher in school-based districts than in districts with centralized management.

No differences were found on the basis of (1) kind of school (elementary vs. secondary), (2) kind of school and type of program (school based vs. centrally managed), (3) kind of school and position (administrator vs. teacher), or (4) kind of school, type of program, and position. Neither respondent state nor school-district size significantly affected the results.

Perceptions of Presidential Leadership Behavior and Institutional Environment by Presidents and Vice Presidents of Selected Four-Year Colleges and Universities in Florida

Rodney James Plowman
School of Education
University of Mississippi
University, Mississippi
Doctoral Dissertation: May 1991

Objective. To assess the leadership practices of college presidents and to determine whether a college's institutional environment is significantly related to its president's leadership practices.

Methodology. The sample consisted of the 9 state-supported, 4-year public institutions that make up the State University System of Florida (SUSF) and the 20 private, 4-year institutions that make up the Independent Colleges and Universities of Florida, Inc. (ICUF). Surveys were returned by 7 SUSF presidents (78 percent) and 18 ICUF presidents (90 percent). In each case, each of the president's administrative team members (vice presidents responsible for academic affairs, business and finance, student affairs, and institutional advancement) were also surveyed. Of the vice presidents, 23 SUSF and 59 ICUF members completed surveys (82-percent response rate).

The presidents completed the LPI-Self, and the vice presidents completed the LPI-Observer. Both groups also completed an institutional-environment (organizational-effectiveness) survey based on the *Excellence Audit* produced by The Tom Peters Group. This 30-item survey focused on people, leadership, and systems.

Key findings. The presidents' perceptions of their leadership practices were all significantly higher than the perceptions of their administrative team members. The presidents generally rated themselves in the 70th percentile or above, compared to all others in the normative LPI profile (generally private-sector executives). The presidents also rated their institutional environments more favorably than did their vice presidents.

There was no statistically significant relationship between the presidents' leadership assessments and perceptions of institutional environment. However, there were consistent, significant relationships between the vice presidents' views of their presidents' leadership practices and the institutional environment. Higher LPI-Observer scores were significantly associated with higher institutional-environment (organizational-effectiveness) assessments.

Hospital Administrator Leadership Practice Before and After the Implementation of Federal Cost Containment Policy

Jay T. Roundy
School of Public Affairs
Arizona State University
Tempe, Arizona
Doctoral Dissertation: May 1991

Objective. To examine the way in which hospital administrators change their leadership behaviors as a result of change in their hospital environments.

Methodology. The sample consisted of 84 CEOs from a random sample of 250 CEOs obtained from the roster of the American Hospital Association. The LPI was used to "provide a practical and understandable description of these [transformational] behaviors" (p. 50). The CEOs described their leadership practices prior to the Medicare Prospective Payment System (PPS) in 1982 and after the implementation of that system. The typical hospital was rural (58 percent), independent and community based (62 percent), with 153 beds. The typical hospital executive was a 46-year-old, well-educated (80 percent had graduate degrees) male (92 percent), with 11+ years of CEO experience.

Key findings. The pre-PPS composite leadership score (all 30 LPI items) was significantly lower than the post-PPS score, indicating that "executive leaders perceive that their use of transformational leadership behaviors increased after the implementation of Medicare PPS" (p. 130). Three leadership practices—Challenging the Process, Enabling Others to Act, and Modeling the Way—were also significantly higher after the change.

Number of years in position and educational level were not significantly correlated with any of the leadership practices. Age was negatively correlated with Inspiring a Shared Vision, Modeling the Way, and Encouraging the Heart. No hospital characteristics (hospital type, type of ownership, medicare certification, or urban/rural) were correlated with the composite leadership score or with Challenging, Inspiring, Enabling, or Encouraging. Modeling was significantly correlated with medicare certification.

"The study findings," says Roundy, "support the conclusion that hospital administrators changed their leadership behavior toward a transformational model since the implementation of Medicare PPS. . .and. . .the change in leadership behavior was not positively correlated with either institutional or personal characteristics" (p. 143).

Superintendents' Leadership Behaviors Which Promote the Instructional Leadership of Principals

Carol Holmes Riley
College of Graduate and Professional Studies
University of La Verne
La Verne, California
Doctoral Dissertation: June 1991

Objective. To determine possible differences between California superintendents' and principals' perspectives of leadership requirements and behaviors.

Methodology. The sample consisted of 83 superintendents participating in the California Advanced Academy for Executive Leadership. Each superintendent identified 3 principals considered to be instructional leaders. The LPI was modified for use with this sample by an expert panel consisting of 2 superintendents, 2 principals, 2 assistant superintendents, and the director of the California Administrator Training Center. The resulting modification had two versions corresponding to the LPI-Self and the LPI-Observer, respectively: the *Superintendent Instructional Leadership Support Survey* and the *Principal Instructional Leadership Support Survey*. Pilot testing involved 7 superintendents and 9 principals. Test-retest reliability was .86 for the superintendent version and .79 for the principal version. Seventy-six percent of the superintendents responded (N = 63) and 73 percent of the principals (N = 183). Of the superintendents, 13 were female.

Key findings. There were no statistically significant differences between superintendents and principals on the extent to which they *valued* the behaviors associated with Challenging the Process, Inspiring a Shared Vision, and Encouraging the Heart. Nor were there differences between the two groups on the rank order of the leadership practices: Inspiring a Shared Vision and Enabling Others to Act were chosen most frequently, Modeling the Way and Encouraging the Heart least frequently. For Enabling, the largest differences were (1) that superintendents placed a greater value on "creates a climate of trust" than principals did and (2) that principals placed a greater value on "commits district resources" than superintendents did. For Modeling, the largest difference was that principals placed greater value on "participates in group principal meetings" than superintendents did.

The two groups differed significantly on the *implementation* of the leadership behaviors associated with all 5 leadership practices. The superintendents' (self) scores were consistently higher than those reported by their principals (observers). The highest mean score from both groups was for Inspiring a Shared Vision, followed by Challenging the Process; the lowest mean score from both groups was for Encouraging the Heart. Enabling Others to Act was ranked third and Modeling the Way fourth by superintendents and in the reverse order by principals.

Identifying and Analyzing the Factors Utilized by Superintendents in Achieving Their "Personal Best" in Education

David L. Long
Professional Studies in Education
Iowa State University
Ames, Iowa
Doctoral Dissertation: August 1991

Objective. To identify and analyze the factors utilized by superintendents in achieving their personal best in education.

Methodology. Kouzes and Posner's *Personal-Best Leadership Experience* was modified slightly and sent to 100 superintendents in California, Missouri, Iowa, and New York (52 percent responded). The typical superintendent had been in the position for 8 years in a district of 6,400 students. Inter-rater reliability for coding personal-best cases was .90.

Key findings. "Each superintendent in the study had at least one leadership story to tell" (p. 30). Twenty-five percent of the personal bests were in the category of "improving climate," closely followed by "growth and expansion" (21 percent), then "effective school projects" (12 percent) and "curriculum improvement" (12 percent). The most important contributors to personal-best success were (1) involving others (33 percent), (2) taking risks (16 percent), and (3) envisioning the future (16 percent). The most important leadership strategy was Enabling Others to Act; the remaining four practices, in order of importance, were Inspiring a Shared Vision, Modeling the Way, Encouraging the Heart, and Challenging the Process. No statistically significant relationships were found between the size of the school district and the personal-best endeavors, practices, or strategies.

"The actions of superintendents who achieved their personal best parallel those found in Kouzes and Posner's research. Superintendents apparently utilized similar types of strategies to accomplish their personal best" (p. 75). Superintendents were more likely than CEOs to Encourage the Heart informally (by expressing thanks) rather than formally (with awards and dinners).

Applicacion del Inventario de Practicas de Liderazgo en Gerentes y Empleados de Empresas Mexicanas (Applying the Leadership Practices Inventory on Managers and Employees at Mexican Companies)

Joaquin Contreras Berumen
Universidad Intercontinental (Mexico)
Licenciado en Psicologia
Master's Thesis: December 1992

Objective. To develop a Spanish-language version of the LPI and to examine its reliability as applied to a group of Mexican managers.

Methodology. The sample involved 83 people, including 22 managers and their direct reports (24 men and 37 women). The managers' average age was 37. More than two-thirds of all respondents held university degrees. About 10 percent of the direct reports had been working with their managers for more than 3 years; another 32 percent had been working with their managers for 1 to 3 years. The tenure of the remainder was less than 1 year. (A minimum tenure of 1 month was required.)

Key findings. Internal reliability (standardized Cronbach Alphas) for the five leadership scales ranged from .81 to .89. There were no statistically significant differences between the managers' self scores and their constituents' scores on Challenging the Process, Inspiring a Shared Vision, or Modeling the Way. However, the managers had significantly higher self scores than constituent scores on Enabling Others to Act and Encouraging the Heart, indicating that these two practices were engaged in least frequently by the Mexican managers. Significant differences were not found between male and female managers on the LPI-Self; significant differences were found between male and female constituents only on Modeling the Way (with men giving higher scores than women). Higher scores were generally found on all five leadership practices as a function of the length of time the constituent had worked with the manager. Respondent age did not affect LPI scores. The leadership scores of the Mexican managers were, on average, lower than those of their U.S. counterparts, but in the same relative order.

At least 7 professionals were involved in the English-to-Spanish and Spanish-to-English translations and retranslations of the LPI using an iterative process until complete agreement was reached. As a result of these efforts, the author concludes, ". . . meanings of the LPI in Spanish are valid and reliable among the Mexican population."

An Examination of Leadership Practices in Large, Protestant Congregations

Thomas D. Zook
Department of Counselor Education
Indiana University of Pennsylvania
Indiana, Pennsylvania
Doctoral Dissertation: May 1993

Objective. To investigate how the leadership practices in large Protestant congregations compare with one another and with leadership practices in business enterprises.

Methodology. Pastors of large Protestant churches (2,000 or more in worship attendance) made up the population (N = 213). Each pastor was asked to complete the LPI-Self and to provide information about himself and demographic data about his congregation. A sample of 132 (62 percent) responded; subsequently, 100 pastors were contacted for interviews and 53 consented. The churches were located in 28 states, although most were in Texas and California. The average age of the church was 55 years (range 4–206 years). There were 5 denominational groupings: Southern Baptist (40), other Baptists (10), Assemblies of God (11), other denominations (32), and "non-affiliated" (39).

Key findings. Leadership practices did not vary as a function of these variables: (1) the pastor's tenure, (2) the pastor's status as founder, (3) the age of the church, (4) the ages of church members, or (5) the congregation's size or rate of growth. However, average scores did increase directly with pastor age. The leadership practices varied as a function of denominational affiliation, "with non-affiliated churches scoring the lowest followed by Southern Baptists. The grouping of other denominations scored highest with Assemblies of God and other Baptists being a close second and third" (pp. 154–155).

Overall, "pastors scored higher in each of the leadership practices" (p. 161) than business leaders (no statistical analyses computed). Qualitative analyses revealed that "leaders in churches and business enterprises are similar not only in their values but also in their generic leadership practices" (p. 173). The greatest difference was that church leaders placed a higher importance on interpersonal openness than did business leaders.

"Pastors and business leaders employ a core group of leadership skills which make them effective as leaders regardless of differences in the nature, mission, and goals of the work site" (p. 233). ". . .they challenge their congregations to break out of molded patterns of behavior by constructively confronting them with new paradigms for living which often engender both risk and opportunity. Through their preaching and leadership, they enlist others to a shared vision for the future by breeding enthusiasm and excitement. They invest time in mentoring leaders whom they empower to serve. By their example, they demonstrate expected behaviors by modeling the way. Finally, they arrange for opportunities to celebrate accomplishments, giving their congregation a sense of significance by witnessing the church in action" (p. 235). One final conclusion from the interviews is that pastors are "in love with leading their congregations" (p. 257).

The Leadership Practices and Strategies of Sixty Respected Recreation, Sport, Leisure and Lifestyle Leaders

Barry Mitchelson
Department of Physical Education and Sport Studies
University of Alberta
Edmonton, Alberta, Canada
Recreation Alberta, Winter 1995, pp. 15–24

Objective. To examine the leadership practices of respected leaders from the recreation, sport, leisure, and lifestyle sector and to compare these findings with the results of Kouzes and Posner's leadership framework.

Methodology. A sample of 100 leaders (divided equally) from the not-for-profit sector, public sector, and private sectors was generated from the nominations of 3 prominent and respected leaders. The response rate was 60 percent, with 17 individuals from the not-for-profit sector, 26 from the public sector, and 17 from the private sector. The respondents completed the long form of Kouzes and Posner's *Personal-Best Leadership Experience.*

Key findings. In all cases the leaders were change agents who expressed a variety of feelings about their personal-best leadership experiences: Twenty-eight felt only positive feelings (excited, confident, energetic), 7 expressed only negative feelings (nervous, anxious, not confident, overwhelmed), and 25 expressed both positive and negative feelings. Less than half of the projects reported on were the respondents' own ideas.

Each respondent had a picture of the future destination. Some of the respondents' pictures were specific, concrete, and measurable, whereas others were more abstract and holistic. All emphasized change and improvement. The respondents worked closely with their stakeholders to develop a common vision.

The most frequent strategies mentioned for Enabling Others to Act were (1) providing unconditional support, assuming organizational members were strong and capable; (2) delegating responsibility and authority, recognizing the potential of the members to succeed; and (3) constantly listening to and involving the members in planning. In discussing the development of trust and mutual respect, respondents most frequently mentioned the importance of "walking the talk." Most respondents acknowledged all types of contributions and accomplishments: individual, group, and organizational. For example, they presented mementos, provided recognition, sent cards and letters of appreciation, and gave verbal praise.

"I am convinced," states Mitchelson, "that the fundamental pattern of leadership behaviors as reported by the respected leaders participating in this study are consistent with the findings of Kouzes and Posner. It would appear logical to suggest that if the behaviors between the two groups are consistent that Kouzes and Posner's leadership model is equally appropriate for both groups. . . . As I summarized and analyzed the data from this study, I considered ways of improving the model. However, I could not find a more effective, yet accurate, method of presenting the data from this study. Therefore, I use the model with conviction and enthusiasm in my ongoing teaching and research and during consulting assignments" (p. 23).

Developing Community Leaders: An Impact Assessment of Ohio's Community Leadership Programs

Garee W. Earnest
Program Leader, Extension Leadership Center
Ohio State University
Columbus, Ohio
Program Report: October 1995

Objective. To assess the effectiveness of Ohio's programs in community-leadership development and the impact of these programs on both the participants and the communities involved.

Methodology. The participant group consisted of 67 people currently in the development programs, 36 alumni of these programs, and 7 program directors. Data were collected at the first and final class sessions for 4 programs (1993–1994). The comparison group (N = 9), selected by the program directors, consisted of individuals who were very similar to those in the programs but who had not applied to participate in the programs. All programs were less than eight years old. Class sizes ranged from 10 to 40 participants. The LPI, focus-group interviews (with 6 program alumni groups), and face-to-face interviews (with 7 program directors) were used. More than one-third of the participants were female; almost all were Caucasian (97 percent); three-fourths held professional or managerial positions; nearly two-thirds had at least a college degree; and 87 percent had an annual gross family income of $30,000 or more.

Key findings. For this study, internal reliabilities for the LPI ranged from .57 to .80 for the five leadership practices. Pretest and posttest assessments with the LPI showed that the program participants significantly increased their leadership skills in each of the five leadership practices. Posttest score increases on Challenging the Process were supported by interviews with alumni, who indicated that they were more willing to take risks than before—even to the extent of running for public office. Higher posttest scores on Inspiring a Shared Vision were supported in interview comments dealing with the development of a broader view of community and greater citizen awareness. Comments supporting an increased ability in Enabling Others to Act were about teamwork strategies, fostering collaboration, and developing more extensive networks.

Posttest comments about Modeling the Way were bolstered by comments from the alumni indicating that they were better able to understand, communicate with, and interact with others in their personal and professional lives. Higher scores in Encouraging the Heart were supported with comments about increased self-confidence and an increased ability to support the self-worth of others.

Leadership Styles of School Superintendents and Collaborative Activity with External Publics

Norma L. Ross
Department of Leadership and Counseling
Eastern Michigan University
Ypsilanti, Michigan
Doctoral Dissertation: December 1995

Objective. To determine the relationship between the leadership styles of school-district superintendents and the extent to which they collaborate with external publics in their districts.

Methodology. Superintendents of Michigan's mid-sized public school districts (N = 367) were the subjects. (The survey instruments were pilot tested with 40 respondents, who were subsequently excluded from the population.) The effective response rate was 75 percent (N = 274). The respondents completed the LPI-Self and provided demographic information. They were also surveyed about (1) the extent to which they collaborated with 4 external publics (businesses, social services, community groups, and educational institutions), (2) the extent to which they implemented community-education activities, and (3) the impact of their collaboration.

Key findings. The LPI scores were significantly correlated with overall collaborative activity as well as with collaborative activity in each of the 4 external publics. Similarly, the LPI scores were positively correlated with the extent to which the superintendents implemented community-education activities in their districts. Ross concludes that "Superintendents whose leadership styles reflect more innovation, an ability to articulate the mission of the organization, a willingness to share power, and a willingness to become personally involved with others are also more likely to involve their school districts in collaborative activities with organizations and agencies outside of the school structure" (p. 133).

An Investigation of the Relationships Between Perceived Leadership Behaviors, Staff Nurse Job Satisfaction, and Organizational Commitment

Cynthia Diane Taylor
Graduate Program in Nursing
Bellarmine College
Louisville, Kentucky
Master's Thesis: June 1996

Objective. To determine whether relationships exist between staff nurses' perceptions of their managers' leadership behaviors and the staff nurses' job satisfaction and organizational commitment.

Methodology. The sample consisted of 80 staff nurses in a 934-bed, tertiary-care medical center (40-percent return rate). Of those who responded, 68 percent were female, with a mean age of 35. Fifty-six percent held associate nursing degrees, and 45 percent worked in an intermediate-care unit. Average years as an RN was 9, with 89 percent currently employed full-time and with an average of 6.9 years in the present hospital. The *Minnesota Satisfaction Questionnaire* was used to measure satisfaction, the *Organizational Commitment Questionnaire* to measure commitment, and the LPI-Observer to measure perceptions of the manager's leadership behavior.

Key findings. Job satisfaction and organizational commitment were significantly correlated with all five LPI leadership practices. No significant differences were found in leadership practices as a result of respondent characteristics such as gender, work status (full- or part-time), area of practice (medical/surgical, intensive care, intermediate care, and specialty), educational degree, age, years as a registered nurse, years with the particular manager, or years with the hospital.

"The behavior of managers in leadership roles," says Taylor, "can influence staff nurses to experience more job satisfaction and increase long-term commitment to the organization. Nurse managers can use the leadership behaviors of challenging, enabling, encouraging, inspiring, and modeling to create an environment that will facilitate success for both the staff nurse and the employing organization. This type of environment would also be likely to have a positive influence on the quality and cost of patient care" (pp. 36–37).

FOR HELP

If you find that you need additional help with the LPI or your LPI feedback, contact:

Customer Service
Jossey-Bass/Pfeiffer
350 Sansome Street
San Francisco, CA 94104–1342
Telephone: (415) 433–1740 or (800) 274–4434
Fax: (415) 433–0499 or (800) 569–0433
www.pfeiffer.com
www.TheLeadershipChallenge.com